MUSTANG SUMMER

Mustang Summer

Other titles by Leif Gregersen:

-"Through The Withering Storm" a memoir

-"Inching Back To Sane" A sequel to TTWS

-"Green Mountain Road and Selected Stories"

-"The Base Jumpers and Other Stories"

-"Poems From Inside Me"

-"First White of Winter Poems"

All titles available in kindle and paperback through
http://www.amazon.com

To learn more and get updates, please visit:
http://www.edmontonwriter.com Or visit my blog at:
http://www.valhalla2014.wordpress.com I also post new poetry regularly on Facebook at Valhalla Books

I can be reached via email at: lgregersen@ymail.com feel free to drop me a line

Dedications:

There are so many people from so many places that have contributed to the efforts that led to me writing this book. One person that comes to mind first is Ray Bradbury, who I saw give a speech online about short stories and got me into the whole swing of it. Of course, no writer really accomplishes so much as just standing on the shoulders of greatness, which was once the opening line to a radio show I produced.

Of the people I would most like to thank before anyone else living is Caroline, who has been my best friend and confidant for over 20 years and still can make me laugh and feel special and all those things a best friend is charged with doing.

A close second is Richard Van Camp, whose incredible talent has brought a whole new understanding to my work and whose constant encouragement and love of the game of writing make me want to constantly keep on creating.

Next of course my departed mother and my ever-present father who is of such genius that instead of exposing me to picture books and fairy tales, when I was a young boy he exposed me to chess, classical music and read to my brother, sister, mother and I from Robinson Crusoe and William Faulkner. My parents always kept the house stocked with the classics and I have them to thank for aiming high in my dreams.

Then there are the numerous friends that cared

enough to encourage me to keep on writing. One of my oldest and dearest friends, who I will simply call Ant is way up at the top and then comes Donna, Mira and many others. There is nothing so wonderful as having friends who trust and believe in you. And of course, I can't forget James, a man 20 years older than me who I can also number among my best friends. Last but nowhere near least is Paula who has been a great friend, fantastic editor and a fellow writer who isn't afraid to take risks for what she believes in. You inspire me, all of you!

Leif Gregersen,

September 6, 2014

THE DESPOT

I have often wondered what may have become of the world if Hitler had taken over power. I think the main thing that would have occurred would be that we would experience global warming at a much faster rate than we are now experiencing. My theory about this comes from the fact that Hitler was in fact a vegetarian and often experienced extreme flatulence. No one apparently ever told him that his broccoli-smelling farts smelled so bad so that he would break down and eat a little meat, because hey-he was the dictator of the largest fascist empire the world has ever known.

As far as the global warming part of it, I learned some time ago that cows have a great deal of flatulence and the type of gas they emit is in fact harmful to the ozone layer. I have wondered for some time now if Hitler pursued his dream of global domination because of the fact that his gas must have been really ripe, and since pretty much what he says goes, a lot of other people would be emitted harmful greenhouse gases from their rectum. I once envisioned him in elementary school passing wind in a great conglomerate of noisy fumes that were so bad they stained his underwear.

"Hitler!" I can hear his teacher saying (I think people would have always called him Hitler knowing he would one day lead his master race of German peoples to a spectacular defeat at the hands of people like Montgomery Clift and James Cagney and of course John Wayne who were simply better than him because they had heart and liked a juicy steak now and then to keep themselves regular).

"Hitler, that is the very height of rudeness!" I envision his elementary teachers would talk like Canadian elementary teachers because I really have no other frame of reference. I think the important point though would be that after blasting forth a stinky one I could see all the other kids moving away from poor Adolf, hoping to somehow avoid the stench that he brought into their classes. All this is why I like to have the odd hot dog, chicken on Tuesdays when The Colonel has a sale on and I try and avoid pop because I know that it can cause me to emulate the most evil chancellor this world has known.

MUSTANG SUMMER

Jerry felt like he was born to be behind the wheel of his newly purchased five year-old Mustang with it's V-8 engine and sport suspension. As he pulled it out of the driveway of the small two-bedroom house he rented in a quiet suburban neighborhood of Edmonton he barely had to breathe on the gas pedal to get it to move, and move fast. It was only 7:30am but on this warm July morning in the sun was already out and there was no need for more than just a shirt without a jacket. Jerry was cautious to go lightly on the gas pedal as he navigated the narrow residential streets. Gas prices were getting ridiculous and he wanted this car to last. Not to mention that he had seen at least five accidents happen in these streets thanks to the fact that they were too narrow for cars to park on both sides and still let by two-way traffic, but people tried anyway. He was generally pretty cautious, but now and then he would get a bit of a lead foot, mostly just on the freeway where there was less chance of hitting something or getting a ticket. Besides, everyone knows a little speed now and then can be good for your engine.

Within a few minutes, Jerry had pulled the agile car onto the freeway and stopped at a light, the last one before three miles of open road. Stopped in behind him among heavy traffic, there was a Chrysler with pair of younger guys in it revving up their engine waiting for the light to turn green. Jerry loved to play with people like this. He figured they had pulled in behind him hoping he would go faster than the rest of traffic so they could slide past him and fly down the freeway, but he left the light no faster than anyone else. Within 60 seconds they had fallen into his trap.

MUSTANG SUMMER   LEIF GREGERSEN

The driver of the Chrysler Intrepid that was behind him really wanted to get around him, but Jerry drove the limit, and the people next to him drove the limit, which drove the young guy crazy. They pulled in close and tailgated Jerry in his Mustang and he smiled to himself and pushed a button on his signal light arm causing windshield washer fluid to come spraying out of the wiper fluid hose of the back window of his car and it drenched the Intrepid behind it. The drivers blasted their horns and hit their brakes. Jerry responded by

slowing down even more. Then, when they found an opening in traffic and sped past him, he gave them the finger for no particular reason. There was something about the danger and the excitement of pissing people off that made Jerry not act his age, which was 35.

Jerry got to work that day for his job as a data entry operator for a small company and settled into his routine of punching in endless columns of numbers and letters that someone else would check and someone else would analyze for patterns. It was a tedious job but it paid well, and it was better than some of the construction jobs he had worked before going back to school to do this. After coming back from lunch the receptionist handed him a slip that said someone had tried to call him during his break and that it was important he return the call. Even though he knew who it was and was pretty sure he knew what she wanted, he sat down at his desk and dialed up the number.

"Candace, you're not supposed to call me at work, we talked about this." Jerry said into the phone when she answered.

"Jerry, it's important, I need a couple of hundred for rent. You're the only person I can ask." She replied.

"We've been through this, I'm not social services and I'm not a bank. Why do you keep calling me? You've been asking me for money ever since my mom passed!"

"Jerry, doesn't what we had mean anything?"

"No Candace, maybe it doesn't. Stop calling okay. Why should I have anything to do with you? You kicked me out, and you don't even let me see my kid!" Jerry slammed down the phone onto its cradle. He tried to stem the flow of thoughts of the events of the past year, but they came rolling through his head. Living with Candace, losing his mom. He thought about his mother a lot but he didn't like to dwell on things. It was just weird how often he would be sitting at home and think that he would like to reach out for the phone to call her and then he would have to remind himself she wasn't there anymore.

The rest of the day went fairly smoothly. Jerry finished up his work, then logged off the computer, punched out and made his way back to his car. He was feeling a bit messed up so when he got to the freeway that would take him home, he let his engine loose a little, wound it up to 90 miles an hour and turned up the music on his Bose CD player. Sometimes he wished he could just keep on driving, forget about his nice little house and his big dreams and just play AC/DC and fly down the highway to destinations unknown. He didn't need women like Candace he thought, he didn't need anything but gas money now that he had a decent set of wheels. With any luck, his wheels could get him a better girlfriend eventually.

MUSTANG SUMMER   LEIF GREGERSEN

After pulling off the freeway, Jerry stopped in at a
liquor store and picked up a mickey of vodka. He got home to
a house full of stifling heat, turned on his two fans and opened
up the window, then opened his bottle. He figured he would
knock back a little booze and then take a cab to a nightclub
once he was feeling loose.

Jerry was a few shots into his mickey when a wind
started to pick up outside. It was a nice wind, it cooled the
quiet street he lived on. But then it started. Bang, squeak,
bang, squeak! The house right across the street from him had
been abandoned a year ago and the screen door had opened
and was swinging open and banging shut, disturbing Jerry's
alcohol induced peace.

'Son of a bitch.' Jerry thought. 'How the hell can people
deal with that happening every time it gets windy here?
Screw it, I'm going to deal with this damn thing once and for
all.' Jerry went to his basement, found a screwdriver and then
walked across the street with it with the full intention of
removing the house's screen door permanently.

Jerry couldn't understand why this house had been
abandoned, it was in good repair, no windows were broken.
The lawn was a mess but a day's work would fix that. He
wondered if he could find the owner and figure out a way to
buy it and fix it up. Jerry had heard of a guy who got owners
to lower the price 10% and then write up a note saying he had
given them the 10% in cash as a down payment, and then get
a mortgage. Flipping houses was big bucks if you had the
right buyer. But right now all he wanted to do was fix the
damned banging.

MUSTANG SUMMER   LEIF GREGERSEN

He set to work taking the door off it's hinges and just as he was about to finish the wind lulled for a moment and he heard the sound of kittens mewing. It was coming from underneath the porch, so he stopped and went to look. The first thing he noticed was a horrible smell coming from the space. He finished up taking the door off, left it in the yard and then went home to get a flashlight. In a few minutes he was back and what he saw was kind of gruesome. There were four kittens, and they were huddled up next to a dead feral cat. Suddenly, he had a flashback of his mom lying on her deathbed, how frail she looked, how scared at what the afterlife would be, because she knew she didn't have much time. Jerry reached in and took the helpless kittens out one by one and nestled them in his arm. He didn't really know what to do with them but somehow he couldn't just leave them there. He brought them back to his house and let them lap up some milk.

Jerry called up the SPCA and asked them what he should do. They told him they would accept the kittens, but that it was most likely they would be euthanized, there was no shortage of cats these days. This kind of made him cringe, so he called up a veterinarian in the neighborhood and they told him to keep feeding them and what shots they would need and a basic speech on how to litter train them. They also told him take them in if they showed signs of getting sick.

That night for the first time in ages Jerry went to bed without finishing his vodka. He had spent his whole evening with the four kittens on his lap, watching TV not wanting to drink himself to sleep in case one of the kittens needed him.

Over the next few weeks Jerry had a lot of fun times with his new furry friends. Something about taking care of a

MUSTANG SUMMER   LEIF GREGERSEN

living being made him happier. He even stopped spraying people in traffic that got too close to him. He spent a lot of his extra money on toys for the cats, everything from catnip to a laser pointer that he would project onto the couch and floor and make them chase. Still, it felt like there was something missing. The cats got a little older and Jerry picked out the one he had called Snowy, who had a half white, half black face and was the most playful of the four. Then he put an ad in the newspaper, and after getting them their shots, he let the remaining three go. He was so careful about them having proper homes he interviewed about 10 families before getting rid of just three cats. Each night after that he would come home and get out the laser pointer and make his remaining cat run and scurry and leap at the little dot it projected.

It seemed that Snowy must have known his mother was a feral cat because as he grew up a little more, he would often scratch at the door and let out a moan that almost sounded like he was trying to say "out". Finally, after weeks of this, Jerry let him go, knowing cats could take care of themselves and find their way home, especially when they got hungry. He made sure and gave Snowy the best food he could, his favorite was Hereford corned beef and that was what he got. But three weeks after he started letting him out every day, Snowy didn't come home. At first Jerry didn't feel all that bad, but after a week it started to worry him. He printed up a few posters at work and put them around the neighborhood. He even offered a $100 reward for the cat's safe return. Then one day he got an anonymous phone call.

"Hello, is this the owner of 'Snowy?'" The voice on the other end asked.

"Yes, did you find him?"

11

MUSTANG SUMMER   LEIF GREGERSEN

"I'm sorry, I did. He was the same cat you described, he was hit by a car. I'm sorry."

Jerry couldn't understand the emotions that went through him at first. He felt tired, he felt sad. He felt alone. He fell back into his chair and covered his face with his hand, and though tears didn't come out, he sobbed a little. Then he composed himself, took a deep breath, and for the first time since he had found the four kittens, he went to the liquor store and got another mickey. He brought it home and sat in his kitchen for a long time thinking and staring at the glass bottle he had just got. He didn't like booze that much, in fact he kind of hated it, but it helped him sleep, helped him forget. He just didn't know anymore what he wanted to forget. Without opening the bottle, Jerry took his car keys and went out and climbed into his Mustang.

Jerry drove to a used car dealer just off the freeway and pulled his car up to the main office. He went in and the owner was just closing up shop, he was sitting with one of the salesmen drinking whiskey out of tumblers.

"I came here to sell my car." Jerry said to the owner.

"That's a pretty nice looking car. How much you want for it?"

"I paid $15,000 for it last fall. $9,000 and it's yours."

"I'd be a lot more comfortable at eight." The owner said.

"Eighty-five hundred."

"I think I can do that."

"Can you do that in cash?" Jerry asked.

"Cash is king." He said, and it was done.

After all the paperwork, Jerry took his license plate and copy of the bill of sale and the cash, and the car dealer gave him a ride to Candace's apartment building. He felt very alone as he walked up to the building and buzzed her suite.

"Hello?" He heard Candace's sweet voice, the one he had once thought would be in his ears forever.

"Candace, it's Jerry."

"Jerry, I thought you understood I don't want you coming here."

"Come on, just come down for a minute. I have something to give you."

"This better be good Jerry." In five minutes, she came down and Jerry was elated that she was the same girl he had once loved so dearly. It lifted a thousand pound weight off his head that she trusted him enough to come down and talk. It had been so long since he had seen her, his heart ached with the emotion that rose up in his chest. He felt like he would do anything to win her back.

"What is it you want?" Candace asked.

"I want to give you this." Jerry said, then handed over his stack of cash, all $8,500 of it.

"Where did you get this?"

"You remember how I got some money from my mom's estate? Well, that's what I got from selling the car I bought when she passed."

"What is it you want me to do with this? You can't just buy your way back into my life."

"I figure I owe you that, and besides..." Jerry mumbled a few more words that Candace didn't catch.

"Besides what?"

"Besides, I want to see my son."

"And you think if you give me some money you can just waltz back into our lives. Jerry! Think! How do we know you won't just take off again? How do we know you're being sincere? You're the most unstable person I ever met."

"Something happened to me. I'm sorry I bailed on you, I was just having such a hard time. I couldn't deal with my mom dying and I understand that now. I haven't drank in a while, I'm going to get counseling. I'm serious, I'll do anything." Candace's eyes began to well up with tears. Jerry could tell there was still a glimmer of love left in them. She leaned in and hugged Jerry.

"Oh, sweetie, I knew you would come around. But we have to take it slow. I can't handle another pointless break-up."

"I understand, I know you have a life."

"Why don't we start by introducing you to the most wonderful beautiful little boy in the world. His name is Jeffrey, and he loves everybody he meets. He'll like you especially."

In the next few months, Jerry went to bereavement counseling and when he was doing better, Candace began to go to his sessions with them. It didn't take long for the trust

to come back into their relationship, and Candace moved back in with Jerry. After they married, Jerry found a new source of energy and ambition, and soon was made into a supervisor at work. It was lucky too, because by the next Spring, the small family was growing. Jerry's new position helped him get a mortgage on the house across the street and before long there were two newlyweds, two children and three house cats living there.

MUSTANG SUMMER   LEIF GREGERSEN

STEPHEN HARPER, OUR PRIME MINISTER

Not many people know much about our Canadian heads of state. Just the other day I was in line at the coffee shop inside the public library and behind me was our Prime Minister, Stephen Harper. I was waiting patiently for my coffee and Harper that ass tried to squeeze into line in front of me. I waited until he was near the till and pushed right back in front of him. I think the till clerk was on my side because I ordered a medium Columbian and he charged me $2.25 and then when Harper came up he ordered a medium Columbian and the guy charged him $14.25 and didn't even open up the till, he just put the money right into his pocket and gave back just a fiver on a twenty. Stephen Harper was a bit of a timid person I guess because he didn't say anything, he just accepted the small amount of change he was given and walked over to wait for his coffee. I think if that happened to me I would tell that guy off and maybe even ask for the manager, but for sure I wouldn't have done what Stephen Harper did-paid the bill and said nothing. I guess old Steve being a conservative and this poor till clerk being a minimum wage dude kind of meant something. The clerk, whose name tag said, 'Anferney' gave him a look that seemed to say, "Look man, just take the coffee and be happy I didn't spit in it."

I had a good laugh over the sight of Harper not doing anything to the cashier guy and then was a bit nonplussed when he brushed past me and took the last seat. In the coffee shop. I have never really been sure what nonplussed means but I think I was feeling it that day. Stephen Harper has always been kind of a person who doesn't make his presence known. Still, someone in the coffee shop seemed to recognize him and I stood happily watching as the scene unfolded.

"Hey-aren't you that guy that used to have a late-night talk show. You know the one, it kind of sucked but I watched it every time Letterman wasn't on. What's your name again." Looking a bit put out, Harper replied to him:

"I'm Stephen Harper, I'm the Prime Minister of Canada."

"No, you're that guy on TV. Mel... Mel something. Help me out here."

"Mike Bullard."

"Yeah, that's you. Hey-can I have your autograph?"

"Sure, I'll even use the official Canadian Government pen the Queen gave me."

"Man, you kill me you guys. Staying right in character. Here, use this paper and my pen." The guy handed Stephen Harper a napkin and pen and he signed it.

"What the hell is this?" The guy said. "This signature isn't real!"

"That's because I'm Stephen Harper, Prime Minister of Canada."

"Man, my wife is going to be really surprised I actually met Mike Bullard."

Harper sat there for a little while sipping his coffee looking quite depressed but not saying anything, and I actually kind of felt bad for him, even though I had to stand up

MUSTANG SUMMER   LEIF GREGERSEN

in that little shop to drink my own coffee. Then I remembered
how he had tried to dismantle our health care to buy new
fighter planes for the military and on my way out I bumped
his table and spilled his coffee all over his pants. I stayed for a
while and when he got up I noticed it looked like he had peed
himself. Later that day I ran into Justin Trudeau, son of our
greatest Prime Minister and we had a laugh over the whole
thing as we sat down in MacDonald's and each scarfed down a
milkshake.

BANNACK, MONTANA

The lone figure on a healthy looking black horse paused every few minutes as they ambled along the dry and arid sand and dirt of central Montana. He needed these pauses to drink from his canteen and it greatly bothered him that he hadn't gotten his horse anything to drink but some muddy water from a stream the day before. It was a scorching hot day as horse and rider maneuvered their way down the Montana Trail. The rider wore a Stetson with silver buckles across the rim of the hat and his clothes gave off the sense that he had money. Money to spend on clothes with a proper fit and fine material, money to spend on comfort. When he wasn't drinking from his canteen, his hands kept a tight hold on the reigns that controlled the horse's speed and direction. This grip was not to keep the horse under control, it was to keep his hands from shaking. It had now been four days since he had a drink of whiskey, and for Eb Walker that was too much. He had placed a lot of faith in the idea that he could make the gold mining town of Bannack before he ran out of water or lost his mind. As he sweated in the midsummer heat though, his doubts rose.

Soon the sun left it's position high in the sky and started to dip towards the western horizon. Eb decided this would be a good time to make camp. He rode up to a patch of trees by the side of the trail and dismounted. His first instinct was to roll up a cigarette, but his shaking hands would just waste all of his tobacco before he could lick it and light it. He broke off some dried branches from a fallen tree and with the help of some paper from a bible an ambitious young priest had given him back in North Dakota, he started up a small fire. Once he got that going, he took his canteen and poured some water in his hand and let his horse lick the water out of it.

Then he took and unrolled his blanket, laid it out by the fire, peeled off his leather boots and laid down to rest.

His sleep didn't last long, a few minutes after falling off into oblivion, Eb Walker had the hideous sensation that insects were crawling all over him. He woke up screaming and slapping himself and when that subsided, he lay, half awake and half asleep, trying to wake himself each time he slipped into another hallucination brought on by the DT's. Somehow he made it to sunrise.

He packed up his gear, somehow managed to roll a cigarette, lit it from an ember of his dying fire and mounted his horse again, silently praying that he would make the bustling mining town by nightfall.

Eb didn't know how to react when he saw the town of Bannack come into view as he rode his horse down the trail that afternoon. He had seen mirages before, and he knew this could be one more. But to his elation, this was the real thing. The promised land. The first thing he did was get his horse all the water he could drink, then he took the half-dead animal to the livery stable and then started to worry about his own needs.

There were a couple of taverns in town and he went into the nearest one, and asked for a shot of whiskey, which he downed as soon as it was poured.

"You look like you needed that one. Have another?" The bartender asked. Eb took out a dollar coin and pushed it towards the bartender.

"Leave the bottle." He said.

MUSTANG SUMMER   LEIF GREGERSEN

Two hours later, near the bottom of the whiskey bottle, Eb finally spoke again: "Got rooms for rent in this Tavern?"

"With or without company?" The bartender said and winked.

"Without. I'm a God-fearing man!" Eb replied.

"You're the first one of those I've seen drink whiskey like that. If you want a flop, you can sleep in the spare storage room for a quarter. A proper room is two dollars a night."

"Two dollars? Why in hell do you charge that much?"

"This is a mining town Mister. Everyone here either has Gold or gets paid by those who do. Like I said, drunks can flop in the back room for a quarter." Eb grabbed the bartender by the collar and glared at him, but didn't seem to be able to get any words out. Then he took out his wallet and put down a $10 bill on the bar.

"I trust you'll give me the change when I leave." Eb said.

"Yes Sir, would you like a meal taken to your room?"

"Just breakfast. Eggs and toast. And a beer."

"As you like Sir."

Though it was barely suppertime, Eb got his room key and went upstairs and slept for almost the next 15 hours. He got up, ate breakfast then brushed out his clothes as best he

21

MUSTANG SUMMER   LEIF GREGERSEN

could to clean them and walked downstairs feeling like a new man.

"Barkeep, have you got any cards?"

"What game do you play Sir?"

"For now, solitaire. I need to get the feel of the cards."

"In a couple of hours some boys will likely be here playing poker. If you like, I can introduce you."

"That would be fine my good man. What kind of stakes do you play for here?" Eb asked.

"As high as you want them Sir."

"Excellent." Eb said, and sat down and carefully dealt out a game of solitaire. It was a fascinating thing to watch as he methodically and with finesse laid out all the cards in perfect rows. His eyes were alight as he scanned through each card, each new draw of cards, not missing a beat. The bartender noticed, and, unbeknownst to Eb, made a signal to a man in the back of the room who left for a half an hour and came back with a big, angry looking hulk of a young man with a large wad of tobacco in the side of his mouth. He came in the door, spat a big greasy oyster of goop into the spittoon, then picked it up and brought it over to where Eb was playing cards.

"You play for money Mister?" The hulk asked.

"I've been known to. Allow me to introduce myself, I'm Eb Walker. I hail from Canada."

22

"You don't carry no guns. Why don't you carry no guns?"

"Sorry uh... your name?"

"They call me Lewis. You didn't answer my question."

"Well uh... Lewis... up in Canada we don't have much use for them. We don't have such a wild west like you do. We have the Queen's law. It works pretty good too." The giant named Lewis laughed and let loose another cannon shot of liquid tobacco into the spittoon, and then wiping his chin.

"You ever play poker Mister?"

"Yes, I know the game. Five card stud, deuces wild?"

"Sure, you can deal first." Lewis said. Eb played for the next while, letting the odd pot go, making the odd mistake. After a few hours, more people joined in and Eb seemed to get a little better, he started winning the odd hand. The stakes started going up and Eb ordered a bottle of whiskey and a shot glass. He took a shot, then a half hour later another and then he seemed to forget the bottle was there. Somehow he seemed to know when he should bet heavy and he got better at bluffing.

The game wore on until midnight and a few players dropped out and then it seemed that everyone had gotten a good hand. All six of the players at the table had a good chunk of their money in the pot and then it kept getting raised and all there was left was Lewis and Eb.

"I think you got nothin' Mister." Lewis said, adding a large plug of tobacco to his overstuffed mouth."

"Well, you're welcome to try me. Here, I'll match whatever you've got left. Show me your cards."

"Full house, Aces over Kings." Lewis said, and spread out the hand that by all rights should have won.

"I've got a full house as well, but I only have tens high." Eb said, and Lewis smiled, a little tobacco dribble running down his chin as he reached out to rake in his winnings.

"Yes Sir, tens and deuces. That makes for five of a kind, and unless I miss my guess, that means you lose Lewis." The crowd erupted with laughter and cheers.

"Who in the damn hell do you think you're playing with Mister?"

"Going to have to call you Mr. One Eleven from now on. You've got three ones on your face now Lewis, three lines of tobacco all spilling out of your mouth." With this, the hulk of a man jumped to his feet and reached for his Smith and Wesson six-shot .45 in what seemed like the blink of an eye.

"What the hell did you say?"

"Lewis!" Someone chimed in. "Don't shoot him! He's got no gun, you'd hang for it." The young giant holstered his gun but didn't sit down.

"I think you're a damn cheater Mister Eb. Walker. What do you say to that?"

MUSTANG SUMMER   LEIF GREGERSEN

"I say you're wrong and that you don't know how to play poker."

"If I'm wrong how the hell did you win all those hands? You got x-ray vision?"

"No, I just notice things. Like how you chew your tobacco harder when you have more than a pair and how you tap on the table when you bluff."

"How the hell could you know that?"

"Just by watching."

"I want a chance to win my money back!" Lewis said.

"I won't let you throw any more money at me in this game and I won't loose to satisfy you. I won this money fair. And if you're out of money I suggest you refrain from betting."

"I have a way to do it fair." Lewis said.

"What way is that?"

"Someone lend me $700.00. I'll take this guy down to Joe's up the block."

"That wouldn't be fair. You're the best player in town Fat boy!" A spectator to the game said.

"You shut the hell up!" He said and threw a beer glass at the man. "That's right Mister, you can't cheat at Joe's and you have to give me a chance to win my money back. House

MUSTANG SUMMER   LEIF GREGERSEN

rules says you can't bow out without a five hand notice and if you leave now you break the house rules and forfeit your money!"

"Don't do it Mister, he's good! Give him half your money and he'll back down."

"No, no. If he wants to shoot pool for the money I think I can let him. My nerves aren't so bad." Eb raised his hand which was shaking, then carefully poured a shot of whiskey, drank it and then had another. "Can someone lend Mr. One-Eleven seven hundred bucks?" Eb shouted and looked around.

"I'll cover him." The bartender said.

"Well then it's done. Lets head over to this Joe's place." Eb said and poured one more shot of whiskey and drank it for good measure. Lewis laughed hard and finally wiped his chin.

Joe's tavern was full of smoke from what smelled like good cigars and pipe tobacco. A lot of well dressed men, likely wealthy ranchers and mine owners sat around and watched the four pool tables in the bar that were kept immaculately clean despite all the carousing that seemed to go on in the bar room. The men that manipulated the numbered balls around with sticks and a cue ball didn't seem as wealthy and were a fair bit younger. Likely the well to do ones were there just to watch the excellence on the green wool that these men could achieve. Lewis went up to one table where some younger men were playing and they vacated the table as soon as they saw him. The hunkering ape disappeared for a minute and when he came back he had the fanciest pool cue in likely all the west. It looked like it was made of ash, and it had decorations and fancy designs all over it. Eb walked over to a

MUSTANG SUMMER   LEIF GREGERSEN

rack of cues on the wall and took one without even rolling it on the table to see if it was straight.

"Okay, we shoot a ball to the end of the table and whoever gets their ball closest back to the edge gets to break. After that, the winner breaks." Lewis explained. "Five games, winner takes all."

"So what you are telling me is that if one of us wins three games, they walk away with $1,400.00. Seems pretty simple." Lewis grimaced.

He had looked a bit drunk, but when Eb leaned over the table with his cue to shoot down table and get as close as possible to the end they were shooting from, his eyes seemed to focus, his unsteadiness seemed to go away. He tapped the ball and it went all the way down, all the way back and stopped while it was touching the edge of the pool table. Lewis's shot left him just an inch away, which meant Eb got to break.

Eb walked down to the end of the table, took a close look at the 15 balls racked into a triangle and then walked back, carefully placed the cue ball and then said 'one'. Then he pulled his cue stick back, slammed it into the cue ball and it hit, scattering the 15 balls but sinking the eight ball. Since no other balls went down, that meant he won. A cheer rose up from all the people that had ever lost money from his hulk of a friend.

After that, Eb broke the next balls out, ran five balls and left an impossible shot for Lewis. Somehow he raised his cue up, hit the ball off to the side, and it miraculously spun around the ball that was blocking his shot and he sunk a ball, giving himself another shot. He took it and sunk four of his balls but while he was shooting for the fifth, he hit the cue ball too hard and it ended up sinking. Eb took over and ran all the remaining balls and then sank the eight.

"Two. Want to give in now?" Eb chided. As he said this, the large man looked like he was about to explode.

"No, let's play it out. You have your fun." Lewis said.

"Well, let me go easy on you then." Eb said, and placed the cue ball in the middle of the table, then hit it hard with a jump shot and it landed in the middle of the racked balls and once again, sank the eight." Lewis became livid.

"Where the hell did you learn that trick?"

"Oh, I toured with the circus for a while. Got my $700.00?"

"I got it but you aren't going to get a chance to spend it."

"How so? You going to shoot me?"

"Maybe. I'll follow you to hell to get my damned money back if I have to."

"That's alright, I'm headed there anyways." Eb said.

"Here," Lewis said, handing over the money. "Now I'd like to see you outside."

"Don't forget I'm unarmed my friend."

MUSTANG SUMMER   LEIF GREGERSEN

"You ain't my friend and I don't care if you're unarmed." Lewis said, spitting on the floor. Eb walked out and his benefactor came out after him. Eb walked off towards the livery stable, counting his $1,400.00 as he went.

"Hold it Mister!" Lewis yelled. "I ain't finished with you yet." Eb kept walking. Lewis took out his Smith and Wesson and fired off two shots at Eb's feet. Eb stopped and turned around.

"You better think about what you're doing Lewis." A voice came out of the crowd that had followed them. Eb looked over and saw that it was the Sherriff. "You shoot him and you'll hang."

"Aw hell, I just want my money back. Come on Mister, fork it over."

"It isn't your money anymore Fatso. I won it all fair and square."

"Yeah but you never told me you were that good at cards or pool."

"And you had never played any pool before? That cue of yours is probably worth a hundred bucks!" Eb said.

"Mister!" Lewis said. Eb walked up to him, raised his arm, pointed his index finger at him and made a quick motion like he was pulling the trigger. Just as he did this, Lewis got spooked and went for his gun.

"BANG!" a shot rang out, but to the surprise of everyone, it was Lewis that fell. Dead. He had been shot right in the head. Eb turned around and walked off, then got his horse and rode out of town.

The Sherriff couldn't very well stop Eb, he had never charged anyone with lethal assault with a finger before, but the next day he went out on the street and looked around, tried to get an idea of the angle Eight Ball had been shot from and what he knew of the people in Bannack. Suddenly the answer came to him and he went up to see Casey, one of the working girls in town who lived up in a second story room above the Dry Goods store. He climbed the rickety stairs and knocked on her door.

"Sherriff." Casey said as she opened her door to him. "Took you less time than I thought to figure things out."

"So you're not denying it then? You shot him."

"Would you have preferred I let him kill that old man?"

"No, but I would prefer if you gave me your gun so I can get rid of it and not mess around with pistols at least within city limits."

"That's all you're going to say to me Sherriff?" Casey asked.

"We both know that skunk Lewis deserved what happened and worse. As far as I understand I'm the only one that knows what happened, and I like you more than I liked that oversized tobacco spitting jerk. I know you were the only one who could have pulled that shot off, but why?"

"That big lummox was bothering me and the other girls since he discovered he liked girls. It was just a matter of time before he tried to rape one of us and hurt them bad. He had already forced a couple girls into freebies and smacked them around. He was giving us a bad name in town. People were thinking they could do what they wanted. Now I suppose you're going to want some store credit for this favor. Well you ain't gettin' any. I know your wife too well. But if you come back in a week or so I've got a friend who can be real discreet about things."

"Casey, how could I ever get you in trouble? You're my favorite working girl!"

"Well I'm not going to be a working girl for much longer. I'm retiring from the profession."

"What are you going to do? Become a gold miner? You can't just give up this sort of life. You make good money and you're well taken care of, all in exchange for a few indiscretions now and then."

"You just might be surprised. You just might be surprised." Until he finished talking and left, Casey stood so that the Sherriff wouldn't see the envelope behind her that was from the office of the town of Bannack that contained five brand new $100 bills.

Eb rode off that night and carefully followed directions he had gotten in a letter some weeks back. He went past the mountain peak that looked like a castle, then waited on the far side of a small stream that crossed the Montana Trail. Before too long after the sun rose, he met up with the man who had written him.

"Mr. Mayor, nice to finally meet you."

"Heh heh. I guess it's true about you Canadians. All so damned polite. And man, you must have brass balls old man. That was beautiful! Here, this is yours!" The Mayor of Bannack handed him an envelope with ten crisp $100 bills in it.

"I'm surprised no one thought to get rid of that big arse sooner." Eb said.

"We had wanted to for some time but he was a damn fast gun and had a bag full of tricks and a bunch of men watching his back. Now that we've got him out of the way we can either jail the rest of his gang or at least run them out of town. You should consider coming back to town! With that money you got you could stake a nice claim, make some real money, and the people there will never forget the courage you showed."

"Well, to be honest I would love to, but I've got other plans. Some time before I put in that ad you answered in the Montana Express, I got the travelling bug. I'm off to San Francisco and I want to see Alaska before I'm done with this world."

"But why did you need all that money? You could have been shot just as easily as a fly landing in syrup!"

"Because of these people." Eb said and showed him a picture of a man in a red serge Mountie uniform standing next to a beautiful woman and a young daughter.

"This is you in this picture?" The Mayor said.

"In the flesh. I love this young girl and this woman more than anyone in my life. I just can't stand being around them and my wife never liked that I was a drinker."

"Well God bless you Mr. Walker. I feel like I owe you my life for what you did. I brought you something, maybe it won't be so good for you but what the hell—you only live once." He said, and went to his saddlebags and handed over to Eb two large bottles of whiskey. Eb smiled and saw the mayor off, then soon headed further down the trail where he stopped at a bank and bought a $500.00 bank draft which he sent to his daughter along with signed divorce papers giving over the rights for all their common property to his soon to be ex-wife. When the Mayor returned to Bannack, it wasn't much longer before he married Casey and he remained married to her right up until the mines dried up and Bannack became just another ghost town in the wild west.

MUSTANG SUMMER   LEIF GREGERSEN

FOUND BY THE SIDE OF THE ROAD

"Number five isn't usually this late." Dwight Edward said to his seatmate Cory on the bus he took home from work each workday.

"Ah, you know how things are with all this construction and so on. The city has to catch up on ten years of neglect after doing nothing with our roads."

"Not to mention doing nothing to stop those greedy gas station owners." Dwight said. "If it weren't for the prices they charge I wouldn't have to worry about catching a bus every day."

"What are you having for supper?" Cory said, trying to change the subject.

"Depends what I make for myself I guess. I was thinking microwaved burritos."

"I thought you were married."

"I am, but my wife stopped cooking for me many years ago. She says I complain too much. Do YOU think I complain too much?"

"No, absolutely not. You complain exactly the perfect amount." Cory said, reaching his arm up to ring the bell to signal his stop for the bus driver. "But you are lucky to have someone to talk to when you get home."

"Yeah, I suppose." Dwight said, not mentioning that him and his wife had barely spoken other than arguments in the past six months. "You have a good one eh, I'll see you tomorrow."

"Not if I win the lotto tonight you won't." Cory said and smiled.

"Let me know how that works out." Dwight said.

A few stops later, Dwight's stop came and he got off the bus, giving a friendly wave to the bus driver and stepping down into a neighborhood where he really didn't fit in wearing a white shirt and tie and carrying a briefcase. He walked past a couple of men and heard the words: "Freaking yuppies." As he went past, Dwight smiled at the idea of being described as 'young' as in 'young urban professional' and even liked the idea that he was the source of jealousy to these guys.

"Hey Mister...!" One of the two men said and Dwight tried to ignore them. He figured they either wanted change or a cigarette, and he hated being treated like a convenience store. "Hey Mister... you dropped something." And with that he stopped and looked down at the ground behind him.

"That red thing on the ground-is it yours?" The bystander said. Dwight looked down to see that a small 'point and shoot' camera was sitting on the ground.

"Hey, thanks." Dwight said, and picked up the small, flat camera and slipped it into his pocket, then went back to walking towards his apartment building.

MUSTANG SUMMER   LEIF GREGERSEN

Dwight got home and as he opened the front door, he wanted to shout, 'Hi honey I'm home' but there was no point. Their small, eggshell colored two bedroom apartment which had no balcony and a view out the window of another apartment across the alley was a cold and unfriendly place. He came in, took off his shoes and noticed that his wife was sitting and watching TV. He couldn't believe that they had drifted so far apart. They had been so close for their first five years of marriage. Now that they had been married 12 years, they were like total strangers, or even worse, roommates that didn't particularly like each other.

Dwight went into the kitchen, dug out two beef and bean burritos from the freezer, then popped them in the microwave. Then while they were warming, he set down his briefcase and brought out the camera he had 'found'.

The camera seemed to be a pretty good one. It had a zoom feature and a nice shiny crimson red finish to it. It didn't seem to have a brand name to it, the only printing on it said, 'magic' and below that someone had put a small cartoon devil sticker on it. The first thing he wanted to do was to look at what was on the memory card. It would be easy enough to plug it into his computer and have a look. Just as he thought this, the bell rang on the microwave and he took his meal into the spare room where his computer was.

"Dwight opened up the camera and pressed down on the memory card which popped back out far enough for him to remove it and slid it into the card reader on his ASUS PC. Then he maneuvered the mouse to click on the contents of the card and all there was on it was a two-minute video. He loaded it onto his hard drive and then hit play wondering what was going to happen. The video started out showing a cloud of smoke and then it cleared and behind the cloud was a strange looking old man with a beard and a pointed hat with stars and moons on it like a wizard.

"Congratulations on finding my camera." The wizard said as his face moved in an odd twitching fashion. "You have just taken possession of one of the most amazing inventions I have made to date."

It was really strange, it almost seemed that the wizard in the film was aware of him, that he wasn't just talking on a video, he was talking through skype or some other service so that he could see Dwight sitting there. He had no webcam or anything set up so this puzzled him all the more. The wizard went on:

"Having done work for the US government weapons lab in my younger days, I learned some interesting things about illusions and magic. I sit here before you as the world's most effective spy weapon designer in history. I invented this little camera and all I will tell you is that you should never point it at anyone you don't want to get rid of, and that after using it three times you must pass it on or face the consequences." With that, the wizard video ended and Dwight was left more puzzled than before.

'Weapon?' He thought. 'Spies? This seems like too much. I wonder who this old nut is and what this camera is supposed to do. He popped out the memory card, put it back in the camera, turned it on and took a picture of his goldfish. Then, when he looked up at the bowl, the goldfish was gone, even though it had been there just seconds before, he was sure of it.

MUSTANG SUMMER   LEIF GREGERSEN

"Holy crap!" He yelled, then heard a series of bangs on the wall coming from the next room.

"Keep it down in there! My show is on!" His wife Annie yelled, and he felt a flash of fear go through him. It took him a long while to process what had happened, but it seemed to him that this camera somehow had the ability to make living things disappear. "Incredible. The things I could do with this!' he thought, then after wolfing down his burritos, he decided to change and go for a walk.

Dwight got on some jeans and a t-shirt and headed out the door. He walked up to a local pawn shop with the camera and tried to look like he was browsing. There were so many cool things in there, from rare guitars to killer stereos. He was after something a little more though, and he wanted to test out the camera.

"How may I help you, sir?" The old man behind the counter asked.

"I want to pawn this camera, but I'm not sure if it works. Can I take your picture?"

"Absolutely sir, if it makes you happy." The shop owner said.

Dwight pressed the power button on the camera, and when it powered up he pointed and took a picture of the old man. Sure enough, when he looked up, there was no pawn shop owner there anymore. He went up to the front door, turned the "open" sign over, locked it and went to the back where he thought the safe had to be. By some stroke of luck, it

MUSTANG SUMMER   LEIF GREGERSEN

wasn't locked and he grabbed a gym bag and loaded it up with a bunch of gold coins and jewelry and then noticed a VHS recorder was going and he took the tape out and put that in the bag too. Then he just went to the door, turned the "open" sign back over and left, leaving the door unlocked. Then he took the bag full of swag to his bank and rented an extra large safety deposit box and stuffed it full of valuables. He figured he couldn't sell any of it for quite some time so he paid the box up for a couple of months and headed back for home.

Dwight took the next few days off work and went around downtown checking out various places, and soon he figured out another plan. There was an armored car crew that came to replenish the cash in two ATM's at the bank down the street from the office he worked at. He had noticed before that there always seemed to be a window of time when the men were exposed and the back of the truck was open. His plan was simple. He would hide himself in plain sight by wearing a uniform that resembled that of an armed guard, he would cover it up at first with a coat and keep his hat in his gym bag. Then he would walk up, take the men's picture and then put on the hat, some gloves, take off his jacket and load up on cash, no one around the wiser. Even if someone were watching they wouldn't believe what they saw.

The time came for him to carry out his plan and it worked well. By some stroke of fate, one of the guards had left their ignition keys on the back of the truck so he was able to get in and drive off with the, loot, take what he could and then drive it into the river. The company and the police would find it soon enough, but it would make it that much harder for them to find him. All in all, at the end of the day, he ended up with about $30,000.00 in cash. He put the uniform he had used in a garbage can and went back home on the bus, quite a bit richer than when he had left. When he got home he didn't get the bland reception he had expected.

"What the hell is the matter with you Dwight?" His wife, screamed at him the second he came in.

"What-what's going on?"

"You took the week off work. Don't you know we can't afford that kind of luxury? I need $200.00 this week just for my medicines."

"Honey, I think I have found out something that can turn our luck around."

"What? You've got some way to make money by hanging out in a coffee shop? I called your friend Cory and he said that's all you've been doing."

"Just don't worry too much about things. I've got the money issues taken care of. Here, take this $300 and get the best medicine you can find." Dwight said and counted off some of the bills he had transferred to his wallet.

"Fine, okay." Annie said. "I'm sorry Dwight, I've been terrible to you these past months."

"Don't worry honey, I still remember the good times we had when we first got married, when we were in love. All that can happen again, there are some good times ahead if you let them happen."

"Whatever this plan of yours is, I hope you thought it through. Because if it doesn't work, I think it's time we divorced and moved on." These words gave Dwight the sneaking suspicion that Annie had heard her mother's health had taken a turn for the worse and that she didn't want to share any inheritance with him.

"Maybe you're right. But give me a chance for now, okay?"

"Your last chance." Annie said.

That night, Dwight went to bed early and stared up at the ceiling. Maybe a divorce wouldn't be so bad. He would be able to go somewhere else, maybe train for a better job with the money he got. He had always wanted to be an accountant rather than a data entry operator. 'So much opportunity, so many new chances.' He thought.

Dwight slept for about two hours and then he half woke up to the sensation of being hit with something and a lot of loud yelling going on.

"An armored car! You held up an armored car!" Came Annie's screams as she smacked him with the handle of a broom. "What the hell were you thinking?"

"What—what in the world are you talking about?" 'She couldn't know about that.' He thought.

"It was on the news tonight. Someone held up an armored car and killed the guards and took thousands. They showed a video and it looked like you!"

"You don't understand—I have this special camera... they will never find me, they will also never find the bodies. We can start over now, we can have the life we deserve!"

"The life you deserve is behind bars! You know about my father, how he went to jail and died in there. You piece of garbage! To think I was going to give you a chance!"

"But no one has to know. I can stop stealing, I just wanted some money for school. We can have everything..."

"No one has to know! I will know! I'm going to call the police. You have the option to leave, but you'll be on the run if you don't turn yourself in, which I suggest you do."

"Son of a bitch! Do you have to ruin everything in my life! I quit school to get a job so you could stay in University! I worked my ass off and then you got sick and I kept working to support you. How many times could I have given up on you!"

"I'm not sharing a bed with a murderous criminal!" Was all Annie said, and went into the next room. Dwight went to get his bag and got out the camera.

He went into the living room and Annie was on the phone. He powered up, pointed and shot the camera. And in a flash, Annie was gone.

The next day, Dwight stayed in bed. He had a horrible feeling that he had done something desperately wrong. Somehow though, the thought of going to Florida or California with his money and being able to have a new start seemed so

MUSTANG SUMMER   LEIF GREGERSEN

wonderful to him. Around noon, when he finally got up, he heard a nagging voice in his head. It went something like this:

"You're stupid, and lazy. All you ever do is care for yourself." He didn't think much of it, but as he went through his day it got louder. "You idiot. What do you think you have done? Do you think you are some kind of hero? You're a loser."

The voice kept talking, and as each hour passed it grew louder and more abusive. Then he realized. There was something the wizard on the film said, something about not using the camera more than three times. He had just used it twice though, once at the pawn shop and again downtown with the guards. NO! He had used it on the goldfish as well.

The next few days passed and as the voice grew stronger and said more to him he realized it was Annie's voice. She was in his head! How did this happen? Well, how did any of these things happen with the camera? The voice wouldn't stop, even when he tried to sleep. He looked in the medicine cabinet that night and found some of Annie's sleeping pills. He took a couple of them but still only fell half asleep. All night he could hear her voice, her nagging, insane voice berating, belittling him. On and on it went. In two more days he was dirty and unshaven, unable to function. Was this what schizophrenia was like? Maybe I've been crazy this whole time? He began to seriously doubt what was real and what wasn't. Soon, he became so distraught and confused that he took all of Annie's pills at once and laid down on the sofa. Then a knock came at the door.

Bang! Bang! Bang! "Dwight! Are you in there? It's Cory!" Dwight opened the door, but kept looking at the floor.

MUSTANG SUMMER   LEIF GREGERSEN

His eyes were glazed over from the pills, his hair was a mess and he hadn't shaved. "Man, you look like shit!" Cory said.

"I feel like shit." Dwight said. And he swayed back and forth like a drunken sailor.

"Man, you need to find a Doctor." Dwight began to cry. His head felt like it was about to explode.

"I need you to take care of something for me."

"What dude, what? I'll help you in any way I can."

Dwight went into the next room, and came back with his duffle bag and camera. "Take this and smash it. He said, handing over the camera. Whatever you do, don't take any pictures with it."

"I can do that. What's in the bag?" Cory asked.

"Oh, you can have that too. Just don't open it until I'm inside."

"Inside where?"

"Inside the mental hospital you're going to take me to." Dwight said.

"Is it that bad?"

"It's that bad. "

MUSTANG SUMMER   LEIF GREGERSEN

With that, Dwight's eyes closed and he slumped to the ground. Cory shouldered the bag, and helped Dwight to his feet and then drove him to the nearby Emergency room.

After he had his stomach pumped and was able to walk and stand, Cory faithfully took his friend Dwight to the psychiatric hospital where he was admitted right away. At first they thought he had some type of treatable illness, but soon they realized that he was being tormented by voices in his head which they couldn't seem to control with medications or even shock treatments.

Soon after getting him to the hospital, Cory opened the gym bag Dwight had given him and realized that it in fact was Dwight he had seen on the news, and that the money was stolen. Not wanting to be any part of a murder, Cory turned the bag in. Dwight was transferred from the isolation room where he had been sitting for months, restrained to a chair, being fed from a tube to a secure facility. His voices never stopped.

Cory as one last act of loyalty to his friend, smashed the camera and the pawn shop owner and the two guards appeared again, right back to where they had last been seen. The fact that the three of them had been missing for some time continued to be a puzzle. One guard thought he had been taken to heaven and the other guard thought he had been taken to hell. The pawn shop owner also thought he had been taken to hell, and a few years later wrote a book about how hell is in reality a cold place something like Alberta in the winter, but with less warm clothes and houses. He went into great description, and the book ended up doing well. No one ever saw Annie again, and her family put on a search but the last person to have spent any time with her was Dwight, who

MUSTANG SUMMER   LEIF GREGERSEN

was never fit enough to answer questions or to even stand
trial. He found a small amount of solace having nothing asked
of him except that he take major tranquilizers several times a
day and try and scream as quietly as he could, which he did
often.

THE END

THOUGHTS ON SILLY CONSPIRACY THEORIES

I often get offended listening to some of the weird conspiracy theories that float around town lately. One time I was working a night shift around the time that the Hale-Bopp comet was passing near earth. A fellow security guard, whose job it was to check and make sure I was doing my job told me that behind the Hale-Bopp comet was actually a spaceship that was coming to take away certain types of people. I don't remember which types of people he referred to but I think somehow he believed he was one of them. I haven't seen him in a while but I have long been wanting to ask him if he had heard any word from the spaceship lately.

All of this of course comes from sources like UFO Internet pages and Conspiracy discussion groups, and especially late night radio. Security guards are very prone to these kinds of conspiracy theories having to often work night shifts which has the effect of causing their brains becoming quite pliable due to the long boring hours with nothing to do and no sleep. The one theory that bothers me the most is that Lee Harvey Oswald didn't kill President Kennedy back in the 60's. This one really gets my goat.

The reason I know that Lee Harvey Oswald did in fact kill Kennedy is because Lee Harvey Oswald lives just up the street from me and I have never known a more suspicious looking character. Sometimes in the summer he puts on an army jacket and walks over to the local park and sits on a grassy knoll suspiciously eyeing anyone who drives past nearby. I know he is up to something whenever I see him. One time I used my powers of remote viewing to check out his house and there were stacks of books from the Dallas Book depository and a number of old Manlicher Carcano rifles laying around. What could be more perfect proof? The only thing that doesn't make sense is that Lee Harvey Oswald now goes by the name Andrew Milley and has a happy family consisting of a wife and two kids and by no means looks like he was alive in the 60's when the assassination took place. To me this is the proof I needed to show people that there wasn't in fact a spaceship behind the Hale-Bopp comet but in fact a time machine where various people mentioned in the late night radio shows were transported from the times they began their conspiracies to present day, and most of them right into my neighborhood.

There are a few conspiracy icons around. Adolf Hitler lives just up the block and works for the city. He is actually kind of a nice man, much taller in person than the evil dictator many have come to know and respect and he doesn't wear a funny moustache anymore. One time he left the frame of a brass bed in front of his house and I took it and got $50 for it at the recycling depot. Then of course there is Napoleon. Most people would think he is French but in fact Napoleon was Italian. He is getting older and likes to sit with the former heads of the Rothschild family of bankers at the Italian coffee shop on the corner. All in all it makes for an interesting neighborhood, but don't let anyone lull you into a false sense of security, these people can be mean. Once Mahatma Ghandi, now gone white from the sun and wearing a normal suit of clothes came out and yelled at me for teasing his dog. Damn dog barks at me he should expect to get barked back at.

HIGH IN THE ROCKIES

He didn't want to have to do this, but he was at the jagged edge of things. Just a few minutes ago his sister had called and once again a normal conversation turned into a fight. Why she even called him now that their Dad was out of the picture he didn't know. It was almost like trying to get gum out of your hair talking to her, every time it felt like he was making progress things got more tangled up. He made the decision that he couldn't face another two weeks of work in this summer heat. He knew what he had to do, but he hated the idea of having to do it. So he took out some paper and a pen and started writing.

Morris dialed the phone number for his supervisor at work, took a deep breath and prepared himself to speak to him, feeling nervous, even though he had written out a script of what he was going to say. Every time Morris was going to have to have a conversation about something he dreaded he used this method. Sometimes it felt stupid, but it worked a lot of the time. The phone rang four times and then his supervisor answered.

"Jorgensen." was all that was said on the other end of the line.

"Hey boss, this is Morris. Can I book off a couple of weeks starting next Monday?" Morris said the words as he read off the sheet he had written out.

"Couple of weeks? Hell, you can have the rest of your life off if you want it." Morris made no indication of being amused. It a funny thing to say since his boss knew he worked hard and had no other job prospects, but a reaction to a joke wasn't on his sheet. Morris fumbled a little and then said:

"No serious boss, I need some time off. Can you spare me for two weeks starting Monday?"

"Yeah, I suppose. More family problems?"

"Sort of." Morris lied. "I have to sort a few things out."

"Understood. Don't be late tomorrow though, we need to have our machine operators relieved on time."

"Understood. Thanks Jens." Morris hung up the phone and breathed a sigh of relief. He hated asking anyone for anything, especially people in authority over him. But at least he got his two weeks off. It was going to make things difficult for him to do without the money he would have made, but he really didn't care. He would rather be poor than so stressed out he wanted to kill himself. When he started to think about the trip though, he almost wanted to dance for joy at the thought of letting some of the pressure off that had been building these past months he had been working in that damned factory. This should be a life-changing trip, he thought. Two weeks in a mountain paradise and then he could get through anything.

Later that night, Morris dug his framed backpack out of the storage closet in his apartment and began laying out the things he would need. On the very bottom he packed in two sweaters and an extra pair of hiking shoes, along with a pair of sweat pants which he wrapped up in a plastic bag to keep them dry in case they were needed and his regular clothes got wet. Then he started to put in food, some cans, some plastic pouches made to be boiled and opened, ready to eat, and a mess tin for cooking and eating out of. Then came soap, a towel, a toothbrush, matches, paper for fire starting and on and on. His method of packing was taught to him by his dad, years ago. He worked through the process slowly and methodically like a professional soldier preparing for a mission. 'Basically the method was all about taking an imaginary walk through your house' Morris could almost hear his father telling him. 'What you take with you has to replace each room. You brought food, utensils, water, dish soap, matches, all the things that would replace your kitchen. Then you moved to the bathroom and brought toilet paper, soap, a towel, and so on until you could live adequately as though the woods were your home'. It was a good method, it worked well each time he went out, and he went out camping as much as he could, sometimes even in the winter. As he was packing, Morris heard a knock at the door.

"Come in Rolly!" He yelled, knowing the door was open and knowing it was his next-door neighbor.

"Hey Morris. What you up to?" Rolly asked.

"Packing for a trip. How about you?"

"Oh, thought I would come over and see if you wanted to watch a movie or anything."

"What movie you got?"

"It's a classic. 'One Flew Over the Cuckoo's Nest'."

"Sorry man, I hate that movie. Hey-what are you doing?"

"Oh, just getting some coffee."

"Ah, go ahead. I keep forgetting you came from a small town." Morris said.

"Oh, sorry. I should have asked."

"Don't worry about it. Just have some coffee and let me get back to my packing when you're done."

"So where you headed?"

"Up near Jasper, going to rent a canoe and hike a trail my Dad and I used to go on."

"You going to take along bear crackers? I understand there's a lot of bears up there." Rolly said.

"Oh, they don't bother you if you don't bother them."

"Suit yourself. So who you going with then? Your Dad?"

"I think I've answered enough questions for one day! Why don't you take your coffee with you and bring the cup back later okay!"

"Sure, sure, no reason to get touchy. Just trying to be a good neighbor."

"Sometimes being a good neighbor is keeping your nose out of what people are doing." Rolly looked surprised at this comment and left without saying anything more.

That Saturday morning, Morris loaded all his gear into his little red Honda, drove down to fill up with gas, checked his oil and fluids and headed out on the highway filled with the feeling of freedom and happiness he used to get when he was a kid and was setting off on another adventure. He used to love camping so much when he was younger sometimes he would load up a backpack and head right out on his bicycle to a nearby provincial campground. Sometimes going alone bothered him but not enough for him not to have a good time. As an adult though, perhaps his favorite part of a trip was the drive. His car ran well and felt comfortable at highway speeds. As he headed off west on the highway to Jasper National Park, playing a CD of John Denver followed by one from Willie Nelson, he was filled with what John Denver referred to as "Rocky Mountain High".

The miles rolled past and the scenery was incredible. High hills and bridges going over green valleys. Millions of trees of all types and sizes lining the road. Then, at some point before Hinton there were the mountains, seemingly bursting out of the skyline likely sixty miles away just as he came around a bend in the highway. Those far-off grey-blue, white-topped behemoths made Morris marvel at the majesty and power of nature. The mountains were almost rebellious in a way, jutting forth towards the sky. This was where he most liked to be on the planet, this was the one place he felt good, not back in Edmonton cooped up in his apartment or sitting beside a noisy machine in a plastics plant putting handles on pails all day until he went crazy. This was where life made sense.

Soon Morris made it to the park gate of Jasper, paid what he thought was way too much for a two-week pass in the park and then rode down the long road to town past picturesque lakes and awe-inspiring peaks. Halfway there he even got lucky enough to go past some mountain goats by the side of the road and took a few snapshots of them.

It was about 2:00pm when Morris finally got into Jasper, and he stopped in at the boat rental place, paid for a canoe, which he would pick up at a lake outside of town, and he was set. No serious plans, no serious commitments, no work, no bosses, just him and the great outdoors for two whole weeks.

He drove out, got his canoe with the key he had been given for the padlock, parked his car, loaded his gear up and off he went through the most beautiful, unspoiled clear green lake he had ever seen. He paddled across the lake, pulled the canoe up on land and started to make camp right away. It wasn't that late, but the sun went down earlier in the Mountains and things cooled off quickly then. Morris had decided he wanted a fresh start early in the morning so he pitched his tent, started up a fire and after a meal of stew and powdered orange juice he took out a book and read until he was tired enough to sleep.

The next morning Morris' eyes opened right at 5:30am. He wanted to stay in his sleeping bag but he heard some rustling outside his tent. He got up and looked out the flap and there was some bedraggled looking man going through his stuff.

"Hey, what the hell you think you're doing?" Morris said.

"I'm looking for the marshmallows." Came the reply.

"Listen buddy, this is my campsite. And that's my stuff. Get the hell out of here." The words didn't seem to phase the stranger, he just kept looking through Morris' gear. Morris got out of the tent and took a closer look at the guy. He had a foot-long beard, unwashed hair, dirty clothes and no shoes. He didn't seem to be a harmful type of person, but he was really out of place in this remote section of the park.

"Hey man-what's your name?" Morris said as he continued pulling out things.

"I'm David. What's yours?"

"I'm Morris, and if you want marshmallows so bad why don't you ask for them?"

"Do you have any?"

"Yeah, in here." Morris rummaged in a side pouch of his backpack and pulled out a bag of marshmallows, then threw them at his new friend.

"Thanks." David pulled open the plastic bag and began popping the sweet treats into his mouth. "If I don't get marshmallows at least once a month I will get too light and float away again." These words puzzled Morris, but didn't worry him.

"I think you should go dude. I want to camp alone." David looked at him funny for a minute, then without a word, the strange visitor retreated into the woods, mumbling to himself and he was out of sight in seconds.

Morris packed up his gear and started off towards the trail he wanted to hike. He thought about his Dad and how much he had meant to him. He wondered what his Dad would do if they had run into a guy like David out in the woods like this. He probably wouldn't have just told him to get lost. As far as he knew, this guy was just sick and had been out wandering for some time and needed help. But Morris tried to push the thoughts of David and what his Dad would do for him from his head and focus on what he came to do for himself: get his thoughts straight after a stressful past few months.

After hiking on for about an hour, Morris started to get the feeling that he was being watched, but each time he heard a twig snap or sensed someone near he would look everywhere and find nothing. Later that day he walked down the trail, making his way higher and higher into the mountains with the blue sky above and the green pine trees and poplars all around him, and he suddenly heard a loud voice say what he thought was the word, "Crap!"

"Alright David, where are you?" Morris yelled as he looked around.

"Here, I'm here. I need some help."

"Okay, I'll help you, just stay where you are and keep yelling."

Morris made his way to David and when he got there the ragged-looking guy was sitting down holding his left leg gingerly, with his yellow teeth gritted.

"What happened David?"

"I stepped on a sharp rock, I hurt my foot." He said.

Morris looked at his blackened foot and, sure enough, it was bleeding something fierce. He took out some water, cleaned up the injured area a bit, poured on a bit of hydrogen peroxide and put a bandage on him. Then, grateful that they fit, he gave David his spare hiking shoes. It was an odd thing to look into David's eyes. He seemed appreciative, but he still had a look to him that was hard to put into words. It was like looking into the eyes of an animal who was never fully tamed. It scared him in a way, but this wasn't the first time he had seen eyes like this. He had a look of craziness to him, but still his eyes portrayed that deep inside of his mind there was a human being, someone good and someone lovable. Morris decided that his Dad would have helped a guy like this get back to civilization and maybe get him some treatment for whatever led him out here in the first place. It just wasn't right to leave a guy suffering like this.

"David, I think I'm going to do you a favor. I'm going to get you out of here so you can get some proper help."

"I don't need no help from nobody." David said.

"There are marshmallows in town. And ice cream."

"Last time I went to town they sent me to the hospital in Edmonton."

"Well, this time if you go I'll visit you. How's that?" Morris hated making promises he would never keep, but he felt somehow obligated to put the guy at ease.

David started to breathe heavy and looked scared. "I don't want to go back Morris. You don't know what it's like!"

"Yes I do know what it's like. You just have to see a Doctor for a while then get some pills. You don't have to live like this. What if something happens to you out here and no one is around?" He almost couldn't believe he was doing this. Normally he wouldn't care at all about this sort of thing. Certainly in the city he would have considered this someone else's problem, at the most tell the authorities in town about David and let them deal with it. But as Robert Service said in his poem, The Cremation of Sam McGee, "There are strange things done in the midnight sun but the trail has it's own stern code." There was just no way he would leave him out here.

After some more convincing, David agreed to go back to town to clean up and get his foot looked at. The foot was tender and there was a good chance it was sprained because he could barely put any weight onto it. Morris left his pack behind and helped David navigate the rough terrain of the trail down the mountain. It was slow going, and they began to talk a lot about what got the two of them to that place, why they were there alone. David talked about some kind of conspiracy of CIA agents trying to kill him and Morris went silent, but then David talked about a mother he had back in Edmonton who had helped him. He asked Morris about his parents and Morris said nothing. As the hours went past, step by painful step, a sort of bond began to form between the two.

Late in the evening, as the sun was starting to dip below the mountains, Morris became slightly inattentive, and as it was darker, he didn't notice that between him and his destination, very close at hand, was a bear cub. He got within five feet of the bear cub and it began to wail something fierce.

MUSTANG SUMMER   LEIF GREGERSEN

Then, it happened. The one thing you don't want to ever see when you frighten a bear cub. The sow grizzly stood up and roared from just 15 feet away in the bushes. David acted fast. He pushed Morris away from him and yelled for him to run down the hill. Then he grabbed a large fallen branch and batted the mother bear. The huge mammal swatted him back and knocked him down but he rolled with the blow and got up almost instantly, ignoring his pain and pushed back the sow, threatening it with his branch. By some stroke of luck the grizzly was only a few feet in front of an embankment and as she stepped back it fell down the small cliff and David was able to hobble, ingloriously, but quickly to safety before the sow returned to wreak more havoc.

David half-ran, half stumbled, his arm bleeding, his foot slowing him down and yelled for Morris. Soon Morris was with him and they moved fast, making it to the canoe in just a few more minutes, urged on by fear and pain. Once they were deep enough into the water, Morris tore a strip from his jeans and used it to bandage David's arm. Then he paddled as fast as he could across the lake while it was nearly completely dark.

Morris got David to the hospital in Jasper and then went and collapsed in a bed in a nearby hotel. The next morning he got up, went and bought some clothes for himself and for David and drove to the hospital to visit his new best friend. When he got there he could barely recognize the guy, he had been shaved and had his hair cut, he had been given a bath. Luckily not too much damage had been done when the bear had swatted him though he needed a few stiches, both in his foot and in his arm. Morris stood over him not wanting to disturb him but somehow he sensed Morris was there and opened his eyes.

"How you doin' there buddy?" David said, as though nothing had happened.

"You saved my life David. How do YOU feel?"

"I think I'm a little sick of fighting bears to be honest. You bring any marshmallows?" Morris laughed.

"No, but I'll get you some. How long are they keeping you here?"

"Just a couple days they said. I think that Doctor is in the CIA and I told him that. He said they were going to send me to Edmonton to the Psychiatric Hospital."

"It won't be so bad David. I know people who were there. I'll come and visit you, bring you marshmallows. You must have a list of movies you haven't seen that came out recently. It'll just be a rest, and I promise you if you don't like thinking normal after you try it out for a little while, I'll take you back here myself."

David reached out his hand, and though his mouth didn't, somehow his eyes seemed to smile at Morris, and he squeezed his hand hard. Morris excused himself just then to use the bathroom but in fact he wanted to disguise that he had a tear running down his face.

Morris stayed in Jasper until David was okay to be transferred to Edmonton and took him there in his car himself. He stayed with him for much of that day as David went through the admitting process, and then let him go on ahead alone when they took him to his ward.

Morris wasn't sure if he wanted to do it, but he sat down, drank a number of sodas and got up enough courage. He remembered the number of the ward, the one he had been given three years ago when the worst thing in his life had happened. If things hadn't turned out the way they would with David he would have never had the courage. He walked up to Ward 10-2, knocked on the door and a Psychiatric Nurse came and opened up the door for him.

"Hi, I'm Morris. You probably don't know me, I'm visiting for the first time. I just wanted to see if... Um... I just wanted to see if Micheal D. is still here. He's came in here three years ago and I haven't seen him yet."

"And you are?"

"I'm Morris, I'm his son."

PEELINGS

It is kind of an odd thing to come to learn about, but I have done it. I have become a connoisseur of fine pubic hairs. I don't mean to imply that I eat them, although there were times when I ticked off the people at McDonald's so bad that I suspect I may have. One should never really talk into the speakers at the drive-through box very quietly, causing the listeners to turn up their volume control and then talk extra loud. I once knew a guy who had a CB radio with a speaker on the outside of his car and he would often order for other people. That may have earned him a special place in the hearts of young McDonald's staff as well, but I digress.

It all started some years ago when I lived in places where you had to share soap. I found that quite often you couldn't really tell what color of hair a person had because their short and curly ones were almost always a shade of red or brown. Certain people, for example full blooded natives of East India often had the hair from their nether regions rather straight and the same color as the hair on their head. As far as our own aboriginal people I don't know, but I can assure you the hair is just as disgusting when you find a bit wedged between your teeth or embedded in the soap you buy for yourself especially after a girlfriend or roommate is careless with their hidden shamefulness.

That is the main reason I decided to start this diatribe. Although I had one roommate who would go to the bathroom without his pants on and leave a drip drip drip behind him upon his return to his bedroom, that wasn't nearly as bad as buying special Ivory soap for the 99 44/100ths percent purity and finding in it a curly black hair the proper length of which, plus the curliness of which leaves nothing to the imagination. For now though, I will simply have to deal with it and pluck each hair I see out of my soap and somehow hope that the soap still gets my hands clean. I do get him back though, I often shower with his green soap since it has such a nice smell to it and I can really use odor suppressants in some of the six main areas of the body that one needs such scents for.

The last tale I will relate is of the time I came home to an apartment I was sharing years ago out on the coast to discover my roommate (who was twice my size and much older) was using the only dish we had, my cereal bowl, as an ashtray. I thought since I was supposes to not mind this he wouldn't mind if I peed in the mess tin he used to heat water on the stove with. He wasn't impressed.

PRINCESS

"Sandra!"

"Yes Mom."

"Time to get out of bed honey." Sandra's mom said as she looked at her beautiful 13 year-old daughter and her strawberry blonde curly hair. The little scamp was trying to get in a few more winks before getting ready for her day. "You're beautiful princess, but you still have to brush your hair and teeth and get changed for school." Her eyes opened, revealing hazel brown eyes that were so pretty anyone could understand why her mom called her 'princess' so much.

"Okay mom, I'll get up now." Sandra said as she lifted herself up and shooed her mom out the door so she could shut it and change. She put on a simple emerald green blouse and a pair of cargo jeans and then went to brush her hair and teeth as told.

Sandra's mom made toast and oatmeal and set out some jam for her baby, her only girl and the light of her life. Soon, Sandra came out of the bathroom smiling and bubbly as always.

"Mom, I can't eat all that sugar stuff." She said. "I'm getting fat as it is."

"Darling, you're five foot four and 95 pounds. That is not fat. You need more food, more sugar because you're still growing. Have toast without the jam and don't add any sugar to your oatmeal if you feel that strongly. But eat!"

Sandra sat down with a half-pretended huff and spooned some oatmeal into her mouth. She played with it a bit but ended up eating it all. When the bowl was almost empty, she ate one slice of toast and then grabbed her books and headed for the door.

"Just wait one minute young lady." Her mom said.

"Oh, sorry mom." Sandra said and went back to the kitchen of their small house and kissed her mom goodbye.

"That's better. Now have a fun day at school. Just nine more days to go before summer." With that statement, Sandra lifted her free arm and cheered and broke into a huge grin that lit up her face. All her mom could think was, 'oh heaven help us when she discovers boys.'

The next nine days went by quickly. Sandra spent most of them studying for finals, but a little time socializing. There was a young man named Derek in her school and a few times she had noticed him looking at her. She wondered what he saw, why he was looking, though she had a pretty good idea.

On their third to last day Sandra was standing at her locker talking with her friends and Derek was down the hall. He stood there for a while, he seemed to be waiting for something, staring at his feet and nervously brushing lint off his shirt. Her bubbly teenage girlfriends told her that he had come up to them and asked if they could leave Sandra alone for a few minutes before the bell so he could talk to her. She was shaking from head to toe, but she stood her ground when her friends went on to their classroom and Derek walked up to her.

"Hey Sandra. How did you end up doing in Science?"

"Not too bad. I got an 89%." She said.

"Not too bad! That course was killer! I only got a 75% and I studied like mad."

"Well, maybe you should study with me tomorrow at lunch." Sandra said and smiled, lighting up not only her own face, but also Derek's.

"That's nice of you to offer, but I was thinking I should study alone. Your pretty eyes would be too much of a distraction." Sandra tried to hide the fact that she blushed deep crimson red at his comment by looking away, but Derek saw it anyway. "I was thinking you might want to grab a movie though, after classes end, sort of a celebration."

"I don't know. I'll have to ask my mom. Would this be a date?" Sandra said with a raised eyebrow.

"A date? No, not a date. Well, maybe sort of... umm."

"It's okay, I think I can go on a date with you. I have known you for all three years of junior high sort of. I'll phone home and ask my mom at lunch and find out if it's okay." As she said this, the bell rang meaning all students had to be in their classes.

"Sure, that would be great!" Derek said. "Here, I wrote down my cell number so you can text me to let me know. I have to get to my class upstairs now though."

"Okay Derek, see you later."

Derek was late for his English Lit class, and even though it was only a couple of days until the end of school, his teacher assigned him to detention. In the middle of his punishment, the text message, 'mom says okay, come to 423 Harcourt Street 5:30 next Tuesday. Bring money for fast food and 2 movie tickets. He texted back his reply and what was left of his hour detention seemed to go like a rocket shuttle launch, and he walked home with his feet barely touching the ground.

That Tuesday, Derek put on a white shirt and tie despite the summer heat and picked daisies in the back alley from his parent's house to bring to Sandra. He went up to her door and knocked and her mom answered. She asked him all kinds of questions, what he wanted to be when he grew up, if he had been on other dates, what was his parent's phone number, and what time they would be back.

Sandra almost had to drag him out the front door telling her mom they were going to miss out on burgers before the movie. She hadn't really known what to expect from Derek, but she liked him, and she wasn't exactly going to marry her first date. She might marry her English teacher on the first date, but that was another case. He had a job and his own money and a passion for literature. From what she understood, Derek was just a plain old boy.

As they walked, Sandra learned more about Derek, and she started to lean towards liking him. He had his own paper route, two of them actually, and he worked on a farm in the summer and was saving up partly for college and partly for his first car. He got good grades but not fantastic. He even picked a good movie and convinced her to eat a salad instead of just a small cheeseburger. He knew a lot about food and nutrition having worked on farms. By the time they went out again the next Tuesday, she had a full-blown crush on Derek. Sandra's mom liked him too and even thought he was cute for such a nerdy boy.

And then it happened.

For the next three weeks, Sandra came home and cried herself to sleep. She barely spoke to her mom, stopped texting or calling Derek and seemed to go around the house like a zombie. One day, her mom came home and Sandra was drinking some beer one of her mom's boyfriends had left in the fridge. She didn't know much about beer; she had just heard that booze could ease a person's pain.

"Sandra, my dear little girl, what are you doing?" Her Mom said.

"I'm having a drink mom." She said.

"But why? What's going on? What has happened to you?"

"I... I can't tell you mom. It's just that..." She broke out in tears and ran into her room. Her Mom followed and went in to sooth her as she put her face down into her pillow.

"Sandra, baby, does this have to do with your new boyfriend?"

"Derek and I went to this park. I don't know what happened. I just drank a pop but for some reason I fell asleep and when I got up I was all woozy. Derek took me home and I was bleeding..." Sandra paused to cry more tears, tears of pain and fear. "I was bleeding down there.."

"Oh my God honey, we have to go to the police."

"But I can't. I'm still not 14. Derek would go to Youth Jail. He probably wouldn't survive it."

"Listen princess, this is no time to be protecting this boy. You can't let someone go free who would do something like this. I'm going to call the police now, and get someone to talk to you who can help." Sandra squeezed out an 'okay' and then ran to the bathroom to get sick.

Over the next few days Sandra had to answer a lot of questions, and she was walked through the basics of what happened with a police psychologist. She felt horrible that Derek had to get into so much trouble but with the help of the youth workers at the police department she found the strength to testify in court. After the trial was over and Derek was sent to a Youth Facility for three years, Sandra's situation didn't get any better.

MUSTANG SUMMER   LEIF GREGERSEN

Sandra would often hold her Mom close until she could sleep and started to drink more and more as time went by. She traded in her fashionable, trendy clothes for fishnet stockings, cut off jeans and a leather jacket with studs. Everywhere she went, she hated everyone, be it school or a prospective job or anything. She soon learned that she fit in better with the punk rock lifestyle than any other.

When Sandra should have finished high school she only had half of the credits she needed to graduate and ended up dropping out in the middle of trying to finish. She found work in a specialty clothing shop for people who were into punk rock, both as a salesperson and a seamstress. She got by for a few years going to parties and nightclubs and working when she could. Soon her whole life was a blur of hangovers and parties with a little work squeezed in. She hadn't even talked to her Mom in six months.

Sandra got older and one day looked back on all the wreckage that had come to her since such a young age and had a glimmer of hope, a moment of clarity that somehow things could change for her. It came in the form of a yellow pages ad for a counseling and addictions service that was funded by the government. She waited up most of the night to call them and caught them first thing in the morning. They set up an appointment for her to do an intake and, by staying up all night before her appointment, she made it into the office bleary eyed and somewhat out of it.

"Hello, you must be Sandra." The cheerful receptionist said to her, forcing a fake smile. She was wearing her punk rocker gear, and if there was one thing the receptionist had noted over the years, prostitutes didn't fare well in this business. She handed Sandra a clipboard with some forms on it. "Please have a seat and fill these out, and we'll get you in to see someone as soon as we can."

Sandra went through the lists of questions and at first didn't want to answer all of them, but her tiredness sent a wave of emotions through her that forced her to keep going. When the forms asked her to list the drugs she had done, she changed the question to which drugs she didn't do and only checked a couple of them off. Then there were endless amounts of true or false questions, which seemed to try and catch her lying. Have you ever wanted to kill someone? Are you a pathological liar? How could they have those two on the same test? Finally, after nearly two hours she had filled in all the forms and actually felt a little better. She handed in the clipboard and papers and sat down again.

In a few minutes, a woman came out and introduced herself as Andrea and asked her to come in. She explained that she had a PhD in Psychology and was more than willing to help. Sandra told her about the drugs and alcohol and all the things that had gone wrong with her life and after a short half hour session Andrea explained that she would love to take on Sandra's case, and that she would like to have her come in for group sessions if she could. Sandra agreed that she would try the sessions and was given a day and time.

On the following Wednesday, Sandra went into the office for her first group therapy session. One person that stood out was a portly looking guy with glasses who seemed very intelligent and wore a comfortable looking brown sweater. Then there was a woman dressed like a male baseball player, and an older woman who looked normal, even better than normal, she looked well off and well educated. Lastly, there was a woman who seemed to try and look into the intentions of everyone in the room by staring them down. Along with them was a lady dressed professionally with a nametag and she introduced herself as the group facilitator. She spoke first.

"Ladies and gent, I would like to introduce Sandra who is with us for the first time. Sandra this gentleman is Paul, the lady to your right is Dana, and these two ladies to the right and left of me are Kathy and Rebecca respectively. Paul, would you like to start us off?"

"Yes, I wanted to say that I have a surprise for everyone."

"Oh, excellent Paul. Would you like to share it with the group?"

"Yes, I've decided I'm going to apply to Law School, as long as they allow me to wear my tin foil hat to classes." Sandra let out a small laugh and everyone looked at her like she had just sworn at a priest.

"Sandra, one thing we try not to do is discourage people by laughing at them. Paul has an issue with radiation and sometimes the only way he feels safe is by wearing his hat." The facilitator said.

"I want to know something." Rebecca interrupted.

"Yes, Rebecca. Go ahead."

"How good is the security in this clinic? I have a concern with people bringing knives in here." She said, and looked straight at Sandra. Her heart sank and she literally couldn't believe someone would say that to her. The odd thing was that she almost wished she had a knife.

"Rebecca, no one is going to hurt you. Everyone here is carefully screened, and we have a security guard I can call at any time."

The session went on for an hour and Sandra actually felt good about it. In a way these were the first 'normal' friends she had made since she was in school. As the session proceeded from those first difficult moments, she learned that Rebecca had been in the military overseas and suffered from Post-Traumatic Stress Disorder and that Paul was a Schizophrenic who had crossed signals firing in his mind all the time.

They were actually pretty nice people. On her way home she stopped at the library and snuck off into a corner with a book of mental illnesses and their causes and read for hours. It seemed as though a lot of the stuff these people went through applied to her. When she was done, she went home and called work and told them she would like to go in the next day.

Sandra woke up the next day and was shaking like mad. She hadn't smoked anything or drank anything the day before and was really in need of an eye-opener as she called them, a couple of beers and a joint to get her through the morning. She decided she was going to try and go clean for one day and went in to work anyhow. Just an hour into her shift, she felt that bed bugs were crawling all over her skin and biting her and she literally let out a scream. Her boss came to see what the commotion was and she was white as a ghost, shaking horribly and looked terrified. She called an ambulance and they came and took Sandra into the University Hospital.

Sandra got a shot to calm down her delirium tremens and was kept for observation for three days. Her Mom came to visit and she looked 20 years older from when she had last seen her. She tried to tell her mom that she was changing things, going to see a therapist and that things were going to improve. Her Mom looked so worried, but said little. She picked up one of Sandra's arms and saw that she had been cutting herself. When she saw this, her Mom began to cry. Sandra sat up in bed, held her and cried herself for a few minutes. The next day to her surprise, she got a visit from Andrea, her therapist.

"Sandra, it is nice to see you." Andrea said as she walked into Sandra's room. "What on Earth has been going on?"

"Well, I thought a lot about things after I went to your office. I decided to try and go clean for a while. Didn't work out too well though. I did like the group though, I want to go back if you will have me."

"Yes of course we will, I just thought it might cheer you up a bit if I came down. I know the Doctor on this ward and he saw in your record you were one of my clients and called me."

Sandra then said, with a bit of nervousness to her voice, "Do you really think you can help me?"

"I know I can Sandra, I know I can. There is something I want you to do though, I want you to look into a 12-step program, I brought you some pamphlets about them, and I want you to try hypnotherapy."

"You want to hypnotize me? Why?"

"Because I think there is something we don't know about you, something you want to get out. You had a terrible trauma as a child, but that doesn't explain everything that's going on with you. Maybe if I can get you to open up a bit, you will be able to feel better."

"I'll do it, I'll do anything not to put my Mom through this until it kills her." Sandra said as tears rolled down her cheeks.

Andrea gave Sandra enough time to go to a rehabilitation hospital for alcohol and drug counseling and then when she got out, she started intensive sessions. Andrea didn't hypnotize Sandra right away; she tried to learn everything he could about her, about how her father had died in a car accident, how things had been growing up, about her first crush.

When they got to that, Andrea stopped and told her to get a good rest and come in for their next session trying not to put pressure on herself or worrying that things weren't going to work. She emphasized that she had hypnotized many people and it had never done them any harm.

The day came and Andrea had a gold pen she held up and rolled around in her hand. She first, rhythmically, methodically, got Sandra to breath slow and deliberate breaths and focus her attention on the pen. Then she did a countdown and brought her from normal awareness to a hypnotized state.

"Sandra, are you there?"

"Yes I am." A little girl's voice spoke in place of Sandra's.

"Sandra, how old are you?"

"I'm thirteen."

"And who is your boyfriend?"

"Derek, he's really cute, he's a great guy too, I love him."

"Now Sandra, I want you to move ahead in time to when you are at the park where you were raped. Tell me what you see." Sandra's face constricted, it seemed to change before Andrea's eyes to a different person and she let out a painful sounding moan. Her breath quickened and she started to weep.

"Oh my God, please don't do this, please, I've never done that before, I really don't want to..."

"Sandra, listen to me, who is doing what?"

"Derek's friend. He gave Derek a beer and he gave me a pop. There was something in my pop, I can't move. Everything is like a nightmare. I feel so tired. I...NO! NO! Stop doing that!"

"What is this person's name?"

"I don't know, he's a hobo, he lives in the ravine. Derek said he was a good guy, that he would watch out for me while he went home for a few minutes, he said he didn't live far but..."

"Okay Sandra, everything will be okay, I want you to imagine the numbers again, I want you to breath slowly, imagine you are at fifteen and are going back to one. Fifteen now, at one you will be fully awake."

Sandra's face seemed to calm but she was sweating and had trouble slowing her breathing down. Soon, she was back to normal awareness and she asked Andrea what had happened. "Did I tell you about the time I was raped when I was on a date at thirteen?"

"You told me something about that, what can you tell me about that now?"

"Well, there was this boy I liked a lot named Derek and we went to a ravine to hang out and I had a pop and he must have put something in it because my memory is blank. He ended up going to jail."

"That's what we talked about, but I don't know if you're ready for what your subconscious mind had to say about all that. There is a very good chance the drug and the trauma changed things around in your head."

"So then what did you do to me?"

"Nothing dear, we just looked over some old memories. If you feel okay, you can go sit in the lobby. Grab some fruit juice before you go for energy though, you went through a lot in this session."

"Okay, thanks Andrea. Take care." In her voice, Andrea could hear a tinge of that same innocent young girl; in her eyes she could see a twinkle of the princess inside of her heart.

Andrea opened her desk drawer and re-wound the tape player she retrieved from inside of it and played it to make sure it got everything. Then she called one of the Sergeants at the Police Department who dealt with sex crimes. In a couple of days they got back to her and had learned that the hobo in question had been found dead a few years after the incident. He had been a suspect, but the evidence was strong against Derek and not the hobo and so they didn't pursue the case. Andrea got him to fax over more information and she spent the next two days pouring over the records.

Andrea learned that the death of the hobo had coincided with Derek's release from Youth Jail. She had no problem with that, but, with the help of the police, she was able to get the address that Derek now lived in. It was a run-down rooming house that made it's rent off people living on welfare or old age pensions. She stepped over a man to get in the front door and went in and knocked on Derek's suite.

"Hi, are you Derek Young?"

"Yeah, that's me. What's it to you miss?"

"I am Andrea. I'm a friend of Sandra's." At the sound of that name, that name that once meant love and happiness to him but had then meant Jail and pain, Derek's right eye twitched and his heart missed a beat.

"All that was over and done with a long time ago." Derek said.

"Derek, all I want to say is that you were wronged. You were done a horrible wrong and I want to help make it right. I hypnotized Sandra while recording her and I now have enough proof that you didn't commit the crime you went to jail for. A public trial would be too messy, and I'm sure there are things you don't want brought up. I've dealt with cases like this before, I've been doing this job for quite a while. I want to talk to someone at the police department and get you to sign a promise not to prosecute for two million dollars."

"And that's supposed to fix what I went through? My teen years gone, my life ruined! That's supposed to mend all the fences."

"You'll have a clear criminal record and a fresh start. I'm sorry, I wish I could do more, but that's a lot better than what some people get."

"Some people deserve what they get. But yeah, if you can do that, I guess I can sign that form. And if you're so god damned sure it will work, write me a cheque for $2,000 right now so I can get a decent apartment. This dive has mice and cockroaches. It isn't fit for a pig."

"I think I can handle that."

Sandra responded well to further sessions, slowly Andrea brought out what happened, and when she was ready, she even was able to give her Derek's number. They talked a little, agreed to meet some time even though they never did. Andrea eventually went back to school to take fashion design and Derek went up to Northern Alberta to buy as big of a ranch as he could. Their lives went on and in ten or twenty years it was almost like they were just regular people again.

STEPHANIE AND MIKE

"Hey I know this level!" Gord said. "You can rescue the Princess from here."

"Only if you take the warp, and it's too hard from here." Mike said.

"Man, you need to take the warp then! We can finish this thing!"

"Finish it? I've finished it a hundred times. This is the oldest Nintendo they made." Mike said.

"Yeah, but WE want to see it, we've been playing this damn thing for weeks. Can't you just finish it to show us?" Gord said.

"Yeah, I suppose I could. Here." Mike said, and maneuvered the video game cartoon blip to the warp tunnels.

"Mike!!" Came a loud female voice from the kitchen.

"Hold on honey, I'm just doing something really tricky." Mike said. And leaned in his seat while he pressed buttons on the rectangular controller.

"Mike I want you to come in here now!" His wife said.

"Just give me a damn second! I'll be right there!"

MUSTANG SUMMER   LEIF GREGERSEN

"I don't know why I keep putting up with this. Sometimes I don't think I want to be here anymore. I'm not happy." Mike's wife Stephanie said into the phone.

"Who are you talking to honey?" Mike shouted from the living room.

"John. He called to ask me what I wanted for my birthday. I told him I want a new chair."

"I can get you a new chair. You don't have to go around asking other people."

"I know, I was just kidding like anyone around here would do anything for me. Can you come in here when you're done though please!" Stephanie said.

"Yes dear." Mike said in a condescending tone. His two fellow video game addicts laughed.

"Holy crap you're gonna do it! I've never seen this before!" Gord said as Mike approached the final dragon guarding the final castle in the video game.

"Not too hard when you've played it five thousand times." Mike said. He finished the game, got his high fives and went into the kitchen, with Gord and their other friend Jake in tow.

"Could you two excuse us for a moment?" Stephanie asked.

"Uh-oh. Looks like Mike's in trouble. We better leave." Gord said.

"No, you guys can stay. Just go in the living room and wait." Mike said.

"It would be better if you left guys. I kind of have something to show Mike." Stephanie said.

"Okay, okay we'll leave. See you later Mike, see you Steph." Gord said.

"See you Mike." Jake said, and the pair went out the back door.

"That was kind of rude." Mike said.

"I just wanted to show you what my sister Stacey sent us in the mail." She opened a cardboard box that was on the table and inside was a slinky red lingerie top.

"Oh, looks pretty nice. It's not really our night for that though is it?"

"Our night? It's never our night lately." Stephanie said. "What's been going on Mike?"

"I don't know, I just kind of feel worn out all the time. Maybe I need some pills or something. I just hate the idea of talking to a Doctor about that kind of stuff."

"I hope you find something soon. I have needs too you know. And they aren't satisfied by rescuing a cartoon Princess."

"I'm sorry honey, let's just wait for the weekend so I can get all rested up first. You know how much my job takes out of me. If things don't work out then, I'll make an appointment with the Doctor." Stephanie stood up and hugged her husband of just 4 years, kissed him and rested her head on his shoulder. It scared her that things had gone this far so soon in their marriage. Just a year ago it seemed they were crazy about each other.

The next day Mike left early for work and when he arrived, went to sanding and polishing slats of wood that he had bought at the lumber yard down the street from the sign shop he worked at. He had found the instructions for his project in a woodworking magazine, and he hoped Stephanie would like it. It was to be for her birthday, it was a hand-made rocking chair. A few years back, when her Dad was alive, she had often marveled at all the hand-made furniture he had constructed and used around the house she grew up in. She had loved her Dad dearly and it left a big hole in her life when he passed away. Now Mike was hoping he could make her some new memories, plus have something soothing to sit and watch TV in. He spent a long time selecting the wood a few months back, and had spent weeks cutting and sanding, measuring and polishing. Her birthday was in just two more weeks so now he had to work on the project every day to get it finished on time.

"Mike, got a job for you." He heard his boss yell from across the shop.

"Sure thing George, I'll get on it in just two minutes."

"I don't know why you're spending so much time and effort on that chair. You can get a better one at a furniture store for a couple hundred bucks." George said.

"Yeah, but this chair will mean something. Besides, after trying to keep a bunch of freeloader friends and a 28 year-old wife happy, I need a hobby. Not to mention that it leaves me broke all the time." George laughed.

"I need you to go do a wall out back of a pawn shop today, better get to it before it rains. Forecast said to expect rain later in the day."

"Sure George, I'll take truck number four." Mike said.

Mike drove downtown to the pawn shop and talked with the owner, making sure he was going to get a good undercoat color for the wall before he lettered it. Funny enough, his old friend John's apartment was right next door to where he was going to do the job. Mike got the undercoat on the wall and then drips of rain started to come down. He decided to pack up and head back to the shop, but he wanted to visit John for a little while, maybe even get a free cup of coffee out of him.

Mike walked up the back stairs and John's window was open so he looked in and when he saw what was inside, he felt like he had just been delivered a knockout punch. There was his wife Stephanie and John, holding each other tightly. All of a sudden emotions of rage and jealousy and betrayal shot through him. All this time John had convinced him, even though he knew her first, that Stephanie and him were just friends. He had always felt she was safe with him. Now he wondered if the whole marriage had been a joke. My God, he thought, what has been going on?

Mike had wanted to break the window glass, scream at John and Stephanie, but he just stood there, feeling like total garbage and then walked off to his truck without doing anything. When he got back to the shop, he just went back to working on the rocking chair and didn't say a thing about what he had seen or what was going on in his mind.

The next few days went by slowly. It seemed that Mike would go home, ignore Stephanie, play video games and drink beer with his friends and during any time he had to spend with Stephanie he was in some kind of quiet rage. He didn't really know what to do, he had taken his marriage vows very seriously. But the idea that because he was having problems that his wife would go to another man just killed him. He didn't understand why he was working, why he was even coming home and paying all the bills while his wife spent his money to sleep with someone else.

Finally, her birthday came and the rocking chair was finished. He put it in the back of his truck, put a tarp over it and drove home, not really knowing what to do with it. He got home and Stephanie wasn't there. He went inside and sat down, pushing himself near to heart attack levels thinking about John and Stephanie together. What had he done wrong? Hadn't he worked himself half to death for four years just so she could try every career from artist to social worker? Hadn't he supported her physically and emotionally? The answer to his question came in the form of a knock on the front door of their small rented bungalow.

MUSTANG SUMMER   LEIF GREGERSEN

"Hello?" Mike said, opening the door to see a man in overalls and a delivery truck outside.

"Hi, are you Mr. Matthews?"

"Yes, that's me. "

"I have a delivery here for you, it's all been paid for, we just have to drop it off."

"What is it? I didn't order anything." Mike said.

"It's a recliner chair, this letter came with it." The delivery person said, handing over the letter. While he went to the truck, Mike opened it and read it.

> Dear Steph:
> I know you would have a hard time getting one of these, but I also know you really want one. I am sorry that Mike doesn't care enough about your comforts to get you a nice chair, so I am taking over the reigns and doing so myself.
> John

"Why that asshole!" Mike said. His first instinct was to smash the chair to pieces, but he held back. "What the hell makes that guy think he can do this to me?"

Mike let in the delivery men, had them put the chair in the living room, then when they left he went out and brought in the rocking chair he had made for her. 'The choice is hers' he thought to himself. She can have that fat old bastard or she can stick with me. It was about an hour before Stephanie got home. All the while, Mike had been rocking in the wooden

MUSTANG SUMMER   LEIF GREGERSEN

chair, getting more and more angry, wondering what he was going to say.

"Hello?" Mike heard Stephanie say when she got in the door. "Mike! Are you home?"

"Yes, I'm in the living room." Mike said. Stephanie walked in to see him sitting in a rocking chair looking angrier than she had ever seen him.

"What's going on Mike? Where did these chairs come from?" She asked.

"Well, the one I'm sitting in was made by my own hands secretly at the shop for your birthday..." Before he could finish, Stephanie chimed in:

"Oh my goodness, it's beautiful Mike! Did you really make it yourself?"

Mike didn't answer, but handed her the letter. She took it and read it and then said:

"Mike, Mike! Don't take this the wrong way. John is just trying to help, he knows I love you! He got some money from an inheritance and wanted to get us something nice. Here, let me show you." She went back into the kitchen where she had set something down.

"He got this for you, look!" She said, and handed him a parcel.

"This is a Playstation four!" Mike said, his eyes aglow. Then all of a sudden he remembered he was angry.

88

MUSTANG SUMMER   LEIF GREGERSEN

"Stephanie, I know you were friends with John for a long time, but I saw something a couple of weeks ago-I was downtown working and I stopped by... You have to tell me, did you sleep with him?" Stephanie began to get tears in her eyes.

"I never told you, I'm sorry. A long time ago we were drinking together and something happened-it was nothing really... but what you saw was nothing. I was just comforting him because he was so upset about his Mom dying."

"Steph, I believe you, but you have to make a decision. I know things have been rough for us, but I love you. I made a promise to spend the rest of my life with you, I think Stephanie, that you have to decide if you want to keep seeing John or keep living with me."

"You can't say that.. You don't understand! He's a wonderful person. What you saw that day was just me comforting him! We didn't.."

"Wonderful person or not, you made a promise, our wedding vows. Love, honor, obey. It's him or me." Mike said, and got up, and walked out the door. "You have two days to decide. And with that, he walked out the door and heard Stephanie burst into tears as he closed it.

Mike kept his promise, he stayed away for two days and went back to the house. He felt all messed up inside, he had so much love for his young wife, she was so amazing to him, in a way he even understood that she cared so much about John, and even thought it was a part of what made her soul and personality so beautiful, not to mention that she was gorgeous on the surface. But he had decided that he just wasn't a man if he could let someone worm their way into his woman's heart like that.

He let himself in the front door, and there was Stephanie, rocking in the chair he had made. The recliner was gone and he breathed a huge sigh of relief.

"Steph, I don't know if I was too hard on you. I love you Stephanie, if you need to have friends, I understand. I just want you to know that it hurts me when things happen like you get an expensive gift from some guy who used to be your lover."

"We weren't lovers. It was just something stupid. But I won't talk to him anymore, I understand how you feel. I told John I wasn't going to see him any more and I sold the chair."

"That thing must have cost a thousand bucks. What did you do with the money?"

"I bought these. I thought it was time for us to have a second honeymoon." Stephanie said and handed him a pair of plane tickets to a resort in Mexico. "And I talked to Dr. Gramlich, he prescribed something that I also got for you." She picked up a prescription bottle from the table next to her and handed it to him as well. "Viagra." She said, and smiled.

"Oh sweetie, you have no idea how much I love you for all this. I just have two questions..."

"What's that..."

"Can we keep the Playstation and do you like the chair?"

Stephanie burst into tears. She thought of her Dad, and what a sweet and gentle man he was, and how proud he would be to have a son-in-law who cared enough about her to craft a chair like this. The pair hugged, and soon they jetted off to Mexico for the best vacation of their lives. Nine months later a little miracle was born and the two raised the child in a happy and emotionally healthy home.

MUSTANG SUMMER   LEIF GREGERSEN

THE VERY GATES

"Hello, Modified Logistics, how may I help you?"

"Hello, may I speak to the person in charge of accounts payable?" Ryan Rogers said.

"That would be Dave Grant, I'll put you through." Ryan hung up the phone and wrote down the name Dave Grant, and reached around behind his computer to turn it on. Once it booted up, he clicked on the word processing icon and then called up a template.

"Dear Mr. Grant" Ryan typed. "It has come to our attention that an employee of yours has run up roaming charges for cell phone account #780-555-2121 in the amount of $492.00 during a recent trip to Las Vegas. This amount is past due and must be paid to avoid termination of service. Please forward a cheque to the above address made out to Rogers as soon as possible. Sincerely, Joe Hayes"

"Beautiful, just beautiful." Ryan Rogers said to himself. He fed the special 'Rogers' stationary into his printer, printed up the letter, then added the letter to an envelope he had previously printed up with his own address which was marked 'overdue accounts', then slid both into an official looking "Rogers Communications" envelope, and put it on a pile with many more just like it. Just as he completed this task, a loud knock came at the door which made him shut off the computer, rush to put his letters away and collect himself before answering the door.

MUSTANG SUMMER   LEIF GREGERSEN

"Carlin, son of a bitch!" Ryan said when he opened the door. "Why in the hell do you knock so loud?"

"What do you do in here that's so secret?" Carlin asked. "You say that every time I come here. Why don't you just put a phone in here so people can call you when you're doing your business?"

"You don't get it do you? The cops can put a tap on any phone, any cell number. You don't even have to pick up a land line and they can hear everything in the room. You think I'm that stupid. I've got a good thing going here."

"You must, you go through more of this nose candy than anyone I supply. Maybe you're just getting into the stuff too much, getting a little paranoid." Carlin said as he eyed his surroundings. "So anyways, the boss said you have some letters to mail and that I should do you a favor so you don't have to leave the house and mail them for you. What's up with that?"

"Nothing Carlin, I just need some letters sent and I can't get out to do it today. Things to see, people to do. Here." Ryan went around to the back of his desk, opened a drawer and took out the pile of letters he had hidden when Carlin knocked."

"You gotta let me in on this Ryan, I've known you a long time. What's up with all the mail and the hiding in this dark little room all day when you got a swimming pool and girlfriends at your place all the time?"

"Well, unless you're pretty stupid you're going to know one way or another soon enough, so I might as well tell you.

MUSTANG SUMMER   LEIF GREGERSEN

See, I got this idea off TV. Some guy over in England went and registered a business that already existed only he registered it in Hong Kong. So then this guy gets stationary printed up and invoices and starts sending out bills to different companies and different people. So I do the same, only it's easier for me because my last name is already the name of a big company. Instead of grubbing for nickels and dimes I send bills to big companies, all I need is the name of the accounts payable guy and he sees the letterhead and just figures everything is nice and legal, and he cuts me a cheque without even thinking."

"You know, if you really pull in the bucks on this," Carlin said, "I might have a need for someone like you. You can be our money man, all you do is provide a little help here and there when we can get a good bulk deal on our products." Ryan always thought it was funny how drug dealers used words like 'products' and 'clients' instead of what they were. Drugs and users. "In return we not only give you preferred rates, you get tons of cash. I'll have to run it by the boss, but we know you're solid, so that would just be a formality. What do you say?"

"I think it sounds pretty good. I was kind of wondering when someone is going to figure out I'm not the owner of Rogers Communications." They laughed. "Besides, I kind of hate the idea of being called "Mr. Rogers anyway. Maybe I will change my name to Mr. Caterpillar. There's a lot of money tied up in those big machines. But seriously, I've got a couple hundred thousand set aside. If your boss wants me in, I'll give it a shot."

"Just watch how much of that stuff you do. The last thing we need is dead friends. You come on board with us and we like to take care of you. We can even get you into the best rehab around if you ever want to clean up."

The two men smiled and shook hands, exchanged pleasantries, and then Carlin left and Ryan sat down and marveled at his good fortune. Then he carefully laid out four lines of cocaine and snorted them with a rolled up five dollar bill. The stuff was pure, not the 80% cut stuff they used for desperadoes. The ecstasy he went through, feeling his heart pounding harder and harder, feeling the rush of adrenalin. He also fantasized himself as some kind of God when he did this stuff. The only thing that sucked was coming down, when he would get paranoid and sometimes hear whispers that he later realized weren't there. He solved this problem by trying to stay high all the time, but it kept on taking more and more of the stuff to do that.

After his pick-me-up snort, Ryan left the dark confines of his den and went out to see that he had house guests. One was asleep on the couch and the other was playing a video game.

"Who might you two be?" Ryan asked, eager to let them know that indeed, all this was his.

"Oh, hey dude. We're Patricia's friends. We got loaded at the club last night and she didn't want us to drive home." Said the young man who had been sleeping up until a minute ago. The other guy, who was playing the game didn't even turn around.

"I see you like to race." Ryan said to the video game player. There was nothing Ryan liked better than playing racing games when he was high on cocaine, feeling the energy of the sights and sounds of the tracks and the simulated fast cars. Not to mention that he could react about ten times better when he was on coke and kick just about anyone's ass at just about any game.

"Yeah man, I love it." The electronic racer said. "I'm Jason by the way. Feel free to jump in with me, we can race each other."

Ryan sat down, grabbed a controller and blasted through computer generated scenery and in and out of lanes of traffic, just barely keeping a lead on his young friend. They played for what seemed like hours and then Ryan asked for a break.

"You two into coke at all?" Jason laughed a stoner laugh when Ryan said this.

"Man, coke rocks. That would be so awesome right now. Pete here isn't into it but then he isn't into anything but women."

"Well Jason, I suggest you and I retire to the den for a little fresh air." Ryan said.

The two went into the den and were gone for a while. Jason's friend Pete couldn't find anything edible in the fridge so he went into the den to see if there was any food around. When he went in, Ryan and Jason were doing lines off the glass coffee table in front of Ryan's desk. They looked up at him through bloodshot eyes and smiled and laughed at him like he had just said something incredibly funny.

"What's up with that stuff? Doesn't it make you push rope when you're with a chick?"

"It can do that," Ryan said. "But at the moment you don't have a chick to worry about those things with and I will add that sometimes it can be a hundred times better than chicks. Give it a try, I guarantee you'll be good to go with the girl of your choice by night time."

"I don't know man. I've smoked pot and shit and even tried crack..."

"Crack my son is a poor man's drug. Coke is for the elite." Ryan said.

"Yeah man, give it a shot. You snort up a little, do a line or two and in seconds you're in heaven man. Nothing like it, all the pain, all the bad shit in your life gone, you feel better than anything you could imagine, just like you just scored the phone number of the hottest chick on the planet."

"Ahhh, maybe I'll try a little. Push over Jase." Pete said and sat down.

The three of them each did a few lines, and Pete got the sudden urge to dive into the pool and swim a couple of laps, but in just a couple of minutes he was back to playing video games with Jason and Ryan. Pete really seemed to get off on the whole racing thrill the video game gave him and the double hit of being euphoric as he raced. As the day wore on, Jason wanted to start drinking and so they sent the girls on a beer and pizza run. Soon the party was back in full swing, more people came over and Ryan started to get pretty drunk. Jason, maybe wanting to show his new rich friend a good time or maybe just being a little stupid, put some LSD into one of Ryan's beers. He drank it without noticing at first, but soon started to trip out.

The music was blasting, the midsummer sun was shining, people were having a good time drinking or getting high. Then all of a sudden Ryan had the sensation that everything was slowing to a crawl. He didn't see the other party goers as people anymore, he felt he could see into their soul. It was like their eyes were the windows and their bodies were just containers of pure love. He stumbled up to Jason, and tried to hug him and said, "I love you man." To him and everyone started to laugh. Just as they began to laugh, they all seemed to turn into frightening demons. He freaked out and yelled a little bit but he seemed to lose the functioning of his legs and kind of 'melted' into the floor. A couple of guys took him into his study and laid him down on the sofa in there and left him talking about the universe and how he could touch the stars, and that they are all love and love is everything...

About a half an hour passed and slowly Ryan began to sense a bit of normality creeping back in, but still his mind was somewhat warped from the acid. He figured the best thing he could do would be to get some more cocaine into his body to jolt him back to thinking more clearly. He didn't know how he got so messed up but he figured a little white powder would get him back functioning so he could party with the people in his house.

Ryan took out the package Carlin had dropped off and opened it. There was a lot of coke in there and he carelessly poured all of it on top of his desk. He was having trouble controlling his muscles and so he just stuck his nose in the pile and breathed in. The coke hit him like a sledgehammer, it

MUSTANG SUMMER   LEIF GREGERSEN

could have been really pure stuff, it could have been just too much. But right after he snorted it, the drug took full effect and he could feel a sharp, stabbing pain in his chest and left arm. He was messed up, but he knew what was happening. He was having a heart attack.

Ryan slumped forward onto his desk and the pain in his chest was unbelievable. He cursed himself for not having a phone in his den, he tried to make himself heard over the sounds of the party outside the room but no one heard him. His felt everything slip away as his heart pounded seemingly out of his chest and the blood became constricted on its' way to his brain.

////////////////////////

Dean never recalled that he had lived a life before this one. All he could remember was being a five year old child, playing with friends and having the most loving parents imaginable. They would read to him, they would play board games with him and all get together every night for supper. His dad worked hard and his mom kept a clean house and drove him to and from school, packed his lunches for him and always made sure he knew he was the light of their lives. Dean grew up and in high school decided he would study art and in University he met a beautiful young woman named Lorna who he could talk with for hours and share everything in his life. One of the things he liked most about her was that she loved her parents and they were just as incredible to her as Dean's parents were to him. When they graduated University, at a ceremony with a few friends and a lot of relatives, they were married. Two years later Lorna gave birth to a blue-eyed baby boy.

Dean and Lorna had great role models who were now grandparents who taught them all the right things to do, plus both of them put a lot of time and trouble into doing the right thing at all the critical times. They taught their baby sign language so he could express himself before he could even talk, they made sure that they had him off the bottle at the right time and when he was old enough they took an active interest in his school. When he was learning to count he got software for the computer to help him. When he was learning multiplication Lorna would grill him with flash cards. They had no exact, laid-out direction for their baby, but they wanted him to have all the options in the world open to him until he was old enough to decide which one he wanted to take.

Time wore on and as their beautiful blue-eyed baby they had named Robin got older, parenting seemed to get more difficult for some reason. The boy would throw fits sometimes, and would not only hit other children at school, he would scream, yell and hit his mother. They kept loving him and kept trying to teach him better ways to act as best they could and hoped it was all just a phase. Sadly it wasn't. Soon he learned how to swear and his parents had no idea where he was getting the words from. When he got to be 12 years old, he was caught stealing and Dean and Lorna tried taking him to see a Psychologist. Then when he was 14 Dean came home early and Lorna was out and Dean caught Robin smoking cigarettes. He didn't get angry, he didn't forbid it, he did what he felt was the best he could do, he talked to Robin about the health risks, told him he didn't have to steal to buy cigarettes and that he would love the boy no matter what. In a year he was doing drugs.

MUSTANG SUMMER   LEIF GREGERSEN

At fifteen the final blow came down. In a fit of anger, Robin punched his mother, giving her a black eye all because she wanted him to turn the TV off and start on his homework. There was no more they could do. They charged him, and with tears rolling down their faces, told him he had to leave.

As the years passed Dean and Lorna heard little of the boy they had loved so much. One Christmas he called up and asked to borrow money to come home to see his parents and his Uncle and they sent the money but he never showed up. Finally, five years after last hearing from him, Dean and Lorna got word that he had died while in jail during a riot. Lorna lost all control and seemed to lose all functioning. Her heart was broken and from then on she only spoke to Dean. She stopped going out, she stopped talking to her friends, even her neighbors. In just that short period of time, Lorna seemed to age a hundred years and passed away herself in just two more.

Dean somehow kept on living, but he developed a problem. He became paranoid and started hearing voices. The voices were calling out to him, but not his own name, they were calling out for someone named Ryan. Some of them sounded like accusing voices, some of them were gentle and peaceful voices that told him things hadn't ended for him, that God still had plans for him yet. He talked to his doctor about the problem and the doctor told him he likely had developed either schizophrenia or early onset dementia. He was given medications and started seeing a psychiatrist who seemed to give Dean more pills each time he went to his office.

One day Dean got up out of bed, took his pills, then fixed himself a breakfast of eggs and bacon, ate them and then went to lay down on the couch to watch morning television.

MUSTANG SUMMER   LEIF GREGERSEN

Then for some reason the voices came really strong, they started to yell, but they were yelling for Ryan. "Come on Ryan, don't do this!" He heard one voice say then he felt a pounding with a sharp pain where his heart was. The pain was really bad and it made him pass out, but when he was under, it all started to come back to him. His name wasn't Dean, it was Ryan. He had an image of people who loved him, he had a sensation that his parents were out there somewhere, but they weren't the kind and loving parents he knew as Dean. It was his alcoholic father who used to beat him and his mother who took him and left to hook up with a string of different men. He wasn't an aging father of a dead young man, a widower with no family, he was a wealthy criminal living off people's trust, but somewhere in the core of who he was there was some kind of good left, some kind of love. His dear Lorna was gone, his life with Robin was a failure. But somehow he reached deep down inside of who he was and in the darkness he willed himself to wake up.

Feeling much like one does when they swim to the surface of a pool after diving far under the surface of the water, Ryan opened his eyes and sucked in a lungful of air, coming back to life. His girlfriend Patty was there next to him and there were two paramedics over him. He realized he had been unconscious and that he had a heart attack and that he was now in an ambulance. Tears ran down Patty's face and he gasped desperately to stay conscious.

"Stay cool Ryan, everything's going to be okay." One of the paramedics said.

"Provided you stop getting high that is." The second lifesaver said.

"I thought I... I was... I was some place else. I wasn't here." Ryan said.

"Just stay cool, you were out for quite a while, you need to relax. We're going to give you some Oxygen now." Paramedic number one said and covered Ryan's face with a mask.

Ryan spent the next few days recuperating and his health returned rapidly. Luckily, his doctor had told him, he had a strong heart and a will to live. When he was released from the hospital, he took a cab directly to the Police Department.

"I'd like to turn myself in." Ryan said to the desk Sergeant when he went in the downtown Edmonton Police Headquarters.

"What kind of crime did you commit?"

"It's kind of complicated. My name is Ryan Rogers, and I registered the Rogers name as a business and fraudulently sent out invoices to companies and was sent cheques which I was able to cash with my ID."

"Crap, wish I thought of that." The desk sergeant said under her breath. "Just have a seat Sir, we'll have someone come down and speak to you.

Ryan spent the next two days in jail and since he wasn't a violent criminal he was released on bail. The first thing he did was walk right to the downtown Detox Centre and check himself in. He went a little antsy going off everything all at once and nearly had a seizure or two, but he

MUSTANG SUMMER   LEIF GREGERSEN

made it through. After a stay there he set himself up to go to the publicly funded rehab and, while he was waiting to go there, he kicked everyone out of his house and put it up for sale. He said little to anyone, never seemed to smile and didn't even thank any of the partygoers for saving his life.

Although he successfully went through rehab, sold everything he owned to pay back the people he had ripped off, there was just too much evidence of illegal activity for the judge to let Ryan off without a sentence. He ended up getting two years less a day, which put him in the Provincial system whereas the harsher Federal system held people who had 2 year or longer sentences, and he served his time mostly keeping to himself, attending church services and mopping floors.

When his jail time was done, Ryan got a job as a janitor with a local school and gave a portion of each paycheque to the church he attended now that he was on the 'outside.' One day by chance he met a teacher who needed help with changing a tire and before he knew it he had his first respectable girlfriend. She was a Christian as well, and inspired him not only to start his own janitorial company, but to give talks at schools and churches and anywhere people gather about what he had been through and the change that had occurred in his life and how it came about. Some people thought he was crazy, some people didn't want to listen to a person who had done all those horrible things. But Ryan would speak to them regardless.

Not too long after that, Ryan married his girlfriend Tina and they had four children, all of whom grew up not ever knowing the things their father did or ever thinking he was even capable of such things. Time passed and their children

MUSTANG SUMMER   LEIF GREGERSEN

grew up, Tina and Ryan one day became proud grandparents and Ryan kept getting up each day to spend his working days running his business and cleaning and his free time speaking, especially to children at risk. He died at a ripe old age of 78, a loved and happy man.

After passing quietly in his sleep, Ryan found himself before Saint Peter and a host of angels. He walked up to where Saint Peter stood with the Lamb's book of life and asked if his name was in it.

"Ryan Rogers, yes, your name is here. This is funny, we almost thought we lost you."

"You mean when I had my heart attack and I was still living in sin?"

"Heart attack? You had a drug overdose and you died. There was nothing we could do. You were in the domain of the evil one. The devil really tried to get you, he took you down to hell, tested you in every way he could. He even had one of his fallen angels pretend to be your son and turn on you. But you got out, you escaped the fires of hell you proved you had a true heart despite that your life hadn't gone well for you. God had a plan for your life, and he has loved you just like you loved your own children. Come past the gates now Ryan, you are finally home."

THE END

MUSTANG SUMMER　　　　　　　LEIF GREGERSEN

TEDDY'S STORY

"Mom, can I get another bowl of frosty bombs?" Tommy Upton said.

"Tommy, if you keep having two bowls of that sugar cereal every morning you're going to get fat. Just look at your father and what happened to him. You know you're at risk for diabetes." Tommy's mom said.

"It's not for me mom, it's for Teddy!" Tommy whined.

"Tommy, I think I need to talk to you. It isn't normal for a 35 year-old man to have a teddy bear like you do. You need to get out more, you need to make some friends your own age. I won't be around forever you know."

"I know mom, but I need Teddy, he keeps me safe. Besides, after I get to New York, everything is going to change for me, you'll see."

"I packed a lunch for you by the way." Tommy's mother said. "I put it in your briefcase in case you have a long wait today at the passport office."

"Thanks mom, that was nice of you." Tommy spoon-fed his teddy bear a few scoops of cereal and then nodded Teddy's head to show that he had eaten enough.

Tommy finished his breakfast and went into the living room of the small apartment he shared with his mother. He

MUSTANG SUMMER   LEIF GREGERSEN

turned on the TV and on the news was a picture of a home computer in the upper corner of screen.

"Today we are going to discuss cyber crimes with researcher Jevan Green. We join him now in our Toronto studios. Good morning Jevan, how are you?"

"Just fine thank you. Had a long night last night getting some spyware off my main system, but ended up sleeping not too bad." The researcher said.

"Can you start us off by telling us what sorts of things someone can do with the data on your computer and how they get in?"

"It's unbelievable really what a good hacker can do really, they can get you to download a Trojan horse virus and then come back later and have full access to all of your files." Tommy went green and shut off the television and rushed into the den where his own computer was kept. He brought his bear with him and was gone for a good hour when his mom finally called him.

"Tommy, you have to get to the passport office now if you want to get all your documents today. Your briefcase is by the door."

"Thanks mom, I'm leaving right away."

Tommy brought Teddy with him and put him inside the briefcase, along with his documents that he needed, grabbed his coat and headed out the door. The passport office was busy, but it didn't take long for the long line-up to die

MUSTANG SUMMER   LEIF GREGERSEN

down and before he knew it, he was sitting inside the office, munching on an apple him mom had packed for him.

"So where you headed?" A young woman asked him who was seated next to Tommy. He was a bit hesitant to talk to her, but this was the kind of thing his mom had wanted him to do, get out and meet people, act like more of an adult. So he took a chance.

"New York." He said.

"Oh hey, that's great. You're going to love it, the city is so full of life." She said.

"You've been there?"

"A few times, I'm a magazine writer and I go just about every year to cover one story or another."

"I'm a writer too. I wrote a book. I'm going to New York to pitch it to a publisher."

"Have you written anything I may have heard of?"

"No, I mostly write children's stories. I tried to self-publish a book but it didn't go all that well." Tommy said.

"Yeah, that can be the case. That's very brave of you to take the intitiave and go all the way to the big apple and all. I hope you do well."

"Thanks, I'm going to try. Where are you headed?"

MUSTANG SUMMER   LEIF GREGERSEN

"Fiji. Three wonderful weeks in Fiji." She smiled broadly and Tommy smiled back.

"Wow, I heard that place is paradise. My Dad took me to Hawaii years ago, everyone there was so nice, and the weather was incredible." Tommy said.

"You should go to Fiji some time, it refreshes your whole soul."

"Mr. Upton!" A voice announced.

"Oh, that's me." Tommy said. "It was nice to meet you."

"You too, all the best in New York."

Tommy walked up, took the forms out of his briefcase and spoke for a while with the passport official. Then he went to another line-up and waited some more. About an hour later, all of his waiting was done and he was told by a clerk his passport would be mailed to him. He walked out with all of his forms and then realized he didn't have his briefcase with him. He stopped in his tracks and ran back inside and couldn't see it anywhere. He looked in all the spots he had been, and asked all the people at all the desks but no one had seen it.

"Teddy!" He yelled. "Teddy! Someone stole my teddy!"

"Take it easy now son, what's the problem?" An aging security guard who was assigned to the passport office said as he walked up to Tommy.

"My briefcase. My bear. They're gone!"

"Your bear?" The guard said with a quizzical look on his face. "What's this about a bear?" Suddenly Tommy realized how crazy he looked, and, out of fear, walked out of the office.

For the next two hours, Tommy walked through the Federal Government building, looking at everyone he could, looking at their briefcases, even looking at their children to see if they had Teddy. Finally, he thought to see if anyone had turned in the briefcase and to his surprise, someone had. He described it for the Commissionaire at the main desk and the guy handed it right to him. Tommy opened the case and his lunch was there but no bear. A look of horror came over him. He went home that day feeling worse than he had ever felt in his life.

"Hello Tommy, how did things go?" His mom said with a concerned look on her face. "You were gone for quite a while, is everything okay?"

"No mom, everything is not okay."

"Why honey, what is going on? Didn't you get your passport?"

"The passport thing went fine, but someone… someone." Tommy choked on his words as they came out. "Someone took Teddy mom, he's gone!"

"Oh Tommy, we can get you another bear, cheer up. You're going to New York soon, you're going to have a fabulous time, don't worry so much about things."

MUSTANG SUMMER   LEIF GREGERSEN

"No, but it's just that..." He couldn't get any more words out and ran into his bedroom and curled up in bed in a fetal position and laid there crying for two hours. His mom didn't know what to do so she simply left some chicken soup by his bed and let him be.

The next day Tommy was woken up by his mom who had a big smile on her face and told him there was a phone call for him. Laboriously, he got up and went to the phone.

"Hello, is this Tommy Upton?" The voice on the other end said.

"Yes, what can I do for you?"

"I'm the owner of a coffee shop in the Federal Building. Someone turned in a stuffed bear this morning and it had a phone number and name on it. Do you want it back?"

"Yes, yes of course. That is so great, thank you so much. I'll be down there in an hour, what's the name of your shop?"

"The Federal Internet Café." The man said, and Tommy said goodbye and hung up. He rushed through his shower and breakfast and headed out the door. In an hour he was at the Federal Building again.

"Hi, I'm Tommy Upton, someone turned in my bear." He said.

"Yes of course, I'm the one that called you." The owner said.

111

"I can't tell you how grateful I am. That bear is the world to me right now." The man looked at him and wondered if he even had any children. He handed over the bear and Tommy gave him a $20 bill. He was glad to get the money as business had been slow and didn't ask any smart-ass questions, despite really wanting to.

In a few weeks, Tommy got his passport, and a short time later he packed Teddy in his carry-on bag and rode the bus out to the airport. For some reason, passing through security, he was singled out to have his bag searched. He went a little red when they did mostly because it was an attractive young woman doing it, but also because he hated the way people looked at him when they learned he had a teddy bear. He got onto his flight on time without hassle and a few short hours later he was in the city that he had only dreamed of and saw on TV.

Tommy wrapped Teddy up in a plastic bag and went down to the lobby with him and had the desk clerk lock him up in the safe. He had heard too much about crime in New York and wasn't going to take any chances. Then he ventured out and saw the Empire State Building, the Statue of Liberty and walked through Times Square. There was much more to see and do but he had an important appointment the next day. When he got back, he retrieved his bear and took him up to his room.

Tommy woke up the next day and put on some expensive cologne his mom had bought him and his best shirt and tie and took out his briefcase, locked Teddy inside and went down to the lobby and had the desk clerk call him a cab.

MUSTANG SUMMER   LEIF GREGERSEN

He made his way in the cab to the publisher's office that he had most wanted to see first, and was asked to come in as soon as he got to the office.

"Tom, pleased to finally meet you." A tall, dark haired and very professional looking man said to him as he entered his office. "I'm John Stanley. We've seen some samplings of your work, it's great of you to come all this way." The neatly and expensively dressed editor said.

"Well, the way things have been going with cyber crime and all, I've been a bit paranoid about trusting the Internet or the postal system. Besides, I have always wanted to see New York so coming here is no problem." Tommy said.

"Okay, so let's see what you've got then." John said.

Tommy placed his briefcase on the table, opened it and took something out and then closed the case and put it on top. His editor knew that there were a lot of crazy people out there, but he didn't think Tommy was one. He had actually brought a teddy bear with him! Damn, he thought, he had liked what he had heard of this guy.

"Do you have a letter opener or a pair of scissors?" My goodness, I hope this weirdo isn't going to try and stab me. Still, there is something about him that tells me he's okay. The editor thought. He opened a desk drawer and brought out a letter opener.

Tommy took the opener and stabbed it into Teddy's stomach, made an opening a couple of inches long and then pulled out a USB stick which he handed to John. He looked at it funny at first, then put it into his computer. He opened the

113

files menu on it and clicked on one that read, "Teddy's adventures in the post office." The file came up and there was a great little story under the title about a bear who mailed himself to different parts of the world and learned about other cultures. It made John chuckle so much at it's beauty and simplicity of style that he told Tommy it was some of the best children's writing he had seen in a long time. There were a number of other stories and he browsed through them and they all seemed equally as good.

"Well, Mr. Upton, I think if I let a few other people have a look at this we can pretty much assure you a contract. That was smart of you to keep your files on a USB like that, you would be surprised at how many things can happen to a computer file. As long as you don't mind, I can make a copy and give your USB back and then in a few days we'll be ready to negotiate an advance. It won't be much, but it will certainly pay for your trip and then some. Thank you for coming down."

"Thank you Mr. Stanley. I have my room booked for another week, you can reach me there."

"We will be in touch then. Take care." Tommy smiled and put Teddy back in his briefcase. "Can you tell me though, how did you manage to get into the mind of a child like this? Some of your writing is amazing."

"Well, I did my research. I started by getting rid of my car and my heavy metal records, and then I moved in with my mother and basically turned the clock back and acted like a child for six months. I'm so relieved this is all over because I think I was actually starting to go nuts."

MUSTANG SUMMER   LEIF GREGERSEN

"I was a bit curious myself at first, but writers can be eccentric at times." John said. "I'm looking forward to working more with you Mr. Upton, you should do very well with us."

Tommy almost couldn't believe his dream had come true, and when he left the office he was walking on a cloud. A contract was soon made up and in eight months a smash hit children's book came out called "Teddy's Adventures" Tommy made enough in royalties to put a down payment on a house for his mom and he ended up moving to New York. Fame and money looked good on him and not long after, Tommy met the woman who would be his wife. After more books and a wedding, they shared a spacious apartment with their baby daughter, two dogs and though he never needed him for much again, Tommy bought a large doll house where Teddy stayed for the rest of his days.

THE FAKE PRINTER

"Kevin, don't you understand that when I married you I didn't sign up for all this, all this poverty and hardship. I could take it if you were working, I could take it if you tried in some way, even if you were on unemployment, but in the past two years all I hear from you is dreams! I'm sick of it, I can't take it anymore." Eliza said to her husband.

"Eliza, baby—I know what I'm doing, I just had a run of bad luck. Things will turn around for me. It's just been tough because of getting the car and putting everything in place. I know I can do this stuff, I've got things worked out."

"Right now Kevin, you have a deadline. You have to get some work, some real work for some real pay in one month or I'm gone."

"Eliza, don't say such a thing. I love you so much, you're my inspiration. You're my everything baby."

"One month Kevin. Now if you want supper, I'm going to make it but if you aren't here I'm inviting Karen over."

"Go ahead, invite her over, I don't mind. I have to check out an auction soon anyhow."

"Oh my stars, another auction! You don't have any money to buy anything Kevin, and you know you always get ripped off there. This is the kind of thing that drives me crazy, you and your little schemes that never pan out. Fine, I'm going to get Karen, do what you like."

Eliza slammed the door to the one-bedroom apartment and walked down the creaky wooden back stairs to her car. She drove an old wreck from the 70's. The car had been one of Kevin's 'gifts' to her when he found out he could get a lease on a new Pontiac with the money Eliza's job brought in. When he heard her car door slam, he went into the bedroom.

Kevin didn't really know what to do to respond to that. He first got a beer from the fridge and sat down in front of the TV. He flipped through the channels and ended up on a religious broadcast. He watched these a lot, sometimes he even got something out of them. On this particular one a preacher was going on about how he had once been enslaved to sin and how he had changed. It looked all nice and dandy, but Kevin had a hard time swallowing it. He saw how these people may have changed, but he also saw that they were probably rolling in donation money and that they didn't pay any taxes on what they earned.

Kevin started to feel restless and edgy. He had these feelings a lot, especially lately. An idea came to him and he shut off the broadcast just as the guy started to really preach about Jesus and salvation. He went into the bedroom and pulled off the knob that sat on top of the bed-post at the head of Eliza's side of the bed and found what he had been seeking, five $20 bills that she had stashed there from payday. He knew he wouldn't get away with it, but then he also didn't care much. He wanted to raise some money and he would need this $100. For some reason it seemed more important for him to have it than her, even though she probably was hiding it to buy him groceries and maybe gas to get to work to

MUSTANG SUMMER   LEIF GREGERSEN

earn more. Something in him said that he really could multiply this money and all would be forgiven.

Kevin raced down the back stairs and jumped into his brand new Pontiac, turned up the stereo, put on his aviator sunglasses, and pulled away with spinning tires off towards the Casino. He stopped at a light and there was a very attractive young woman in the car next to him and he looked at her and smiled. When the light turned green he tore off and loved the fact that he still had the looks to flirt with the younger generation of women. Just as he was about to get to the Casino, his cell phone rang.

"Hello?" He said

"Mr. McCann?"

"Yes, that's me."

"This is the finance department at GM Canada. We haven't received your lease payment this month yet and it's the 5th already. Payments must be made by the 31st in order to avoid further action."

"Yes, I understand. I just had a little setback, I'll deal with it on Monday when I get paid." Kevin lied.

"Very well Mr. McCann, we value your business."

Kevin pulled his shiny black Pontiac into the parking lot at the Casino. Every time he pulled in there he noticed that there was almost always a few hundred cheap looking old cars and just two or three nice ones. He was never going back to driving a piece of junk. Now he had style and class. Now he was driving what he deserved, he thought to himself, even though having the car he drove had very little to do with him.

Kevin went in and sat down at a blackjack table which was empty with a $10 minimum bet and laid out all five of his $20 bills and asked for $10 chips. He had been working on two systems to increase his chances and he figured now the time was ripe for them to pay off. Maybe he could even win enough to get what he wanted at the auction and pay back Eliza. He didn't want to lie to and cheat her the way he had been doing, but he had been raised having everything handed to him even though his family was a mess. He justified being able to do the things he did by figuring that the way he got treated was a fair trade for what he took for himself.

Kevin laid down a $10 chip and the dealer dealt him an ace and an ace to himself. He was given the option of insurance, which would cost half of his bet, which would get him his money back if the dealer hit blackjack. He declined it and then got a jack and the dealer got an 8, meaning blackjack for Kevin, 1.5 times his bet returned to him.

On the next hand Kevin was dealt a 10 and a 3 and the dealer had a king showing. He pretty much had to hit, there was a low chance of the dealer going over 21 and Kevin winning his bet if he didn't. Another card was dealt which was a queen, putting Kevin over 21, which meant he 'busted' and was now down the $10 he had bet. For the next hand, thinking that a loss was almost always followed by a win, Kevin upped his bet to $50. It was a long shot, but that was how Kevin liked to play things. On this hand, he was dealt a 3 and an 8 giving him eleven, meaning a face card would give him a very good chance of winning at 21 (though he wouldn't get blackjack and win 1.5 times his bet because blackjack was always one face card and one ace) Kevin doubled down, meaning he had to put another $50 out and get just one more card and he slammed his hand flat on the blackjack table when he drew a 10 and the dealer drew an 8.

From then on, Kevin was cautious and reserved, carefully hedging each bet, taking no serious chances, and all the little balls seemed to roll in his direction. In two more hours he had inched his way up to $1,000 with his two systems, one of which was increasing a bet after a loss and the other which was trying to keep an eye on which cards were being played. When he reached just over a full thousand he cashed in, and headed out to his car. He checked his phone and there was another message for him from the GM people but he ignored it and headed off for the auction, hoping to buy something that would double his money as he had done a few times before.

When he got to the auction, the items up for sale were the cars in the back lot. He tried bidding on a few of the fancier looking ones but the bidding went way over $1,000 in short order. Then they moved inside and he noticed a few items that caught his eye. The first was an engagement ring with a massive diamond in it. Soon the bidding began:

"What am I bid for this beautiful platinum and diamond ring valued at $5,000? Do I hear $300? Do I hear $300? $300? $300? How about $250. The idea of something so valuable being within his grasp was excruciatingly exciting to Kevin. When the caller said $250, an overweight and balding older man put up his hand and the tennis game began. $300... $300? Do I hear $300 for this beautiful ring? Kevin put his hand up and the bidding went back and forth. Finally at $900 Kevin let it go and decided on trying for something that he could sell a little quicker. Rings sometimes could sit for months before they sell, and pawn shops gave way less for them than they were worth. There were a lot of things in the room, but one box caught his eye, it was a box containing a new Macintosh computer that came with a color printer. This he figured he could get easily and would sell in no time. People loved Macs.

A number of items came and went, then after about 45 minutes of waiting and watching the excitement, the computer came up for bid. The first bid was $500 but fortunately it only went up in increments of $50 from there. This time there were two other people interested, but at $950 the box was Kevin's. He paid the fee and the taxes, and with barely money to fill up his gas tank, he had a couple of the workers at the auction load the computer into his car.

Kevin got into his car and first checked his message which said, "Mr. McCann, this is GM finance, we are very sorry but we are going to disable your vehicle and recover it." Disable my vehicle? How in the heck would they do that? He soon was to find out.

He drove the 10 km or so home and at about the halfway point everything in the car simply went dead. Then he remembered that the salesman who had sold it to him had said that new cars were now able to be controlled by satellite as a safety feature. Safety feature my ass, they just shut my car down! He called a cab and loaded the computer in it and headed for his unhappy home.

"Kevin! What the hell is going on?" Eliza said as he was coming in the door. "Did you take my money? What is that thing you bought?"

MUSTANG SUMMER   LEIF GREGERSEN

"It's a bargain and a half Eliza, I got it at the auction and we'll be able to sell it for at least $2,000. It's a brand new Macintosh computer with a printer and everything."

"You didn't answer me Kevin, did you take my money?"

"Alright, I took your money, but it's really our money isn't it, and look what I got for it."

"The only way you can get something like that for $100 is if it's stolen Kevin. I don't know what has come over you."

"It's not stolen, it's all very simple, I used your money to try out my blackjack system and it worked. I cleared a grand and bought this, which I can get two grand for. We're out of trouble babe, all the bills will be paid as soon as I can unload this." Eliza closed her eyes, and a look of pain went over her face. She not only looked pained, she looked tired, worn out. She didn't know what to say, didn't know what had happened to the ambitious and hard working young man she married who had once shown so much promise.

"Fine, do what you want, but the deal stands. One month to change your ways." Eliza said and stormed out of the kitchen, slamming the door to their bedroom. She knew she wouldn't get rid of him, that she needed him as much as he needed her. She was just sick. Sick of the lies, sick of the shabby apartment, the bed bugs, the mice and the cockroaches. She got her keys and left without telling him anything.

Kevin plugged everything on the computer in, attached all the wires to the keyboard, the mouse and the printer. He couldn't check out how it worked on the Internet because they didn't have a connection in their place. He turned on the computer itself and the printer and when the computer started it gave a message that said for him to click the 'print' button. He did so and what happened next nearly made him soil himself.

The printer clicked and whirred and made a sound like it was printing and then all of a sudden $100 bills came sliding out one by one, making a small pile. Ten of them came out before the machine stopped. He picked them up and rolled them around in his fingers, they looked and felt real, he had no idea how it happened, but it seemed that somehow he had bought himself a counterfeit printing press. In a mad rush, he turned off the computer, put everything away in their boxes and sat down to try and think about what to do next.

To help clear his head, Kevin walked down to the liquor store, and bought a mickey of vodka and then on the way home a tube of toothpaste, paying both times with a $100 bill. The clerks didn't even look twice at the cash, they just took the bills and gave him his change, which was now real money. He went home and drank some vodka, then waited for Eliza to come home, gave her two $100 bills and told her he would never steal from her again and that he was going to get work soon. Not long after, there was a knock at the door.

"Yes, who is it?" Kevin said through the door.

"It's someone that wants to chat. Someone who is interested in that computer you bought." Kevin looked through the peephole at a very mean looking man in his 50's who had slicked back dark hair and had broken his nose at some point in his life.

123

"I actually sold it already." Kevin stepped back and told Eliza to phone the police. "The guy didn't give a name, but I think he works for the Apple Store in West Edmonton Mall."

"Well, if you hear from him, please give me a call." The man said, and slid a business card under the door. "I would be very grateful if I could get it back."

Kevin looked at the card and it was for a Private Detective and it had a picture of a .38 special revolver pointed at whoever was reading the card. A chill went down Kevin's spine when hc wondered what the visit had meant. He asked Eliza to go and lay down for a little while so he could conduct some business and then he went to work setting up the computer again. As soon as he could, he printed off three and a half stacks of bills. He assumed it ran out of paper and so he opened it and to his surprise there were more bills inside. This was too good to be true, but it certainly explained a lot. This printer never could print money, someone had just set it up to look like it did and possibly dupe someone he figured. He was about to feel extremely satisfied with himself but then there was another knock at the door, which made him cringe in complete terror for just a few seconds.

"City Police!" Came a voice from the other side.

"Just a minute, I'll be right there." Kevin yelled, and took all the money he had and rolled it up and stashed it under the sink. Then he went and opened the door and the cops almost pushed their way in.

"We got a report about someone trying to break in."

"Well, the guy didn't try to break in, but he seemed threatening to do something and he slid this card under my door." Kevin handed him the card.

"We've dealt with this guy before, you were right to call us. Can I get your name sir?" One of the cops asked.

"Kevin. Kevin McCann."

"The cop gripped his radio and spoke into it. Do you know what all this was about?"

"He said something about a computer. I just bought one at an auction and I think he wanted it back. I told him I didn't have it anymore."

"What's the issue with this computer? Can I see it?"

"Yes, of course." Kevin said. "Come in, it's here on the kitchen table."

One of the cops looked at it and seemed to recognize it as he let out a grunt. Then he turned the screen around to check the serial number and almost automatically reached for his handcuffs. He cuffed Kevin and started to read him his rights.

The police radio crackled and said something almost unintelligible and then the cop said, "You are being taken in because you have a warrant out for you and you are also being charged with possession of stolen property." He said to the immobilized Kevin.

MUSTANG SUMMER   LEIF GREGERSEN

"Stolen property? I got this at an auction."

"Can you prove that?"

"No, everything there is cash and carry."

"This computer was reported stolen four days ago. We've been out looking for it. Unless you can come up with some proof, you're going to jail for a few months." Eliza had woken up and came out to see what the commotion was and as she stood looking at Kevin with her arms folded, he turned red-faced with shame.

"Look, if it's stolen, can't I just give it back?"

"Too late now. Unless we felt like being nice guys. Do you feel like being a nice guy Jay?" The cop said to his partner.

"I always like to have a little motivation to be a nice guy Doug."

"I think I understand." Kevin said. "Can you take these handcuffs off for just a minute?"

"I guess we could."

"Kevin rubbed his wrists and then went under the sink and brought out $1,000 in hundreds. He counted out five each for the officers."

"Well, I think this is enough to make me feel like being a nice guy."

"I would feel a lot nicer if we didn't have to explain any of this, say if we picked up this guy but had to release him tomorrow when his story checks out and maybe he gives us some information about this cash and carry auction house."

"Good idea. I'm also more comfortable with that seeing as how he had a warrant for an unpaid fine." The first cop said and handcuffed Kevin once again while the other cop picked up the computer.

Kevin was taken to the Remand Centre and put into a holding cell with ten other men and the stink was unbelievable. There were perverts and drunks who had crapped themselves and while he was in there, one guy got violently beaten up by a mouthy teenager who kept talking about how tough he was. The guards did nothing about this and the guy that got beaten up didn't get any medical treatment. Kevin didn't get a wink of sleep, he kept thinking if he closed his eyes someone would poke a dirty HIV infected needle in his arm or do something evil to him. In the morning the guards came and got them and one by one they went to see a judge. Kevin was released after agreeing to pay his fine, but he had been totally freaked out by the experience. He had always had a home, always had some power over what went on in it. In this holding cell he was horribly affected by all the things his mind manufactured that could have happened to him.

Kevin walked home and when he got to his apartment the door had been kicked in. He went to the bedroom where he heard a noise and there was Eliza, curled up and crying her eyes out in the corner.

"Th… they kicked the door in Kevin." Eliza said through tears. "I thought they were going to kill me. They kept asking about the computer and I told them the police had it, one of them hit me. They said if I didn't tell them everything they would rape me." Kevin's heart sank as these words came out of the mouth of the woman who had stood by him and somehow loved him despite all he had done. He had felt violated himself, but now he felt even worse, angry and frustrated that he couldn't stand up to anyone. Powerless that he was arrested, powerless that he had gotten messed up with these crooks. He held his wife for a good half hour and then went to get her some juice to give her some strength and while he was there he checked under the sink and the money he had hidden was still there. He was hungry, he was tired, he hadn't slept, but he spent the rest of the day nursing and soothing Eliza. Finally, later in the day she calmed down and had something to eat and could talk.

"Kevin, you have to tell me what's going on. I don't care how bad things are, there are ways to make a change, it's never too late."

"Baby, I'm so sorry. I can't believe I brought all this on you. Those guys, they were really bad men, con artists, and they had some money tied up in that computer-literally. I didn't know them, I just bought the computer thinking I could resell it, I swear. I don't know if they will be back, but they might, they will likely try and kill me. Pack a bag, we're going to get on a bus and head South. We're going to start fresh and I'm not going to do any of this stuff anymore, no more auctions, no more stealing, no more gambling. I love you, all I want is you and our life together to work out. I have a little money, enough to get us started."

"We have to get rid of that money Kevin. Don't you see we'll never be free from those men or any of this stuff if we keep taking dirty money? We can go to Lethbridge, stay with my sister for a few weeks, that's all the help we need if we can find work."

"Okay baby," Kevin said. "I want you to go some place you feel safe and I'll go get a pair of bus tickets."

"I'll be at the Assumption Catholic Church."

"Okay, I'll meet you there then we'll come back together and pack."

Kevin felt all jumbled up inside. He felt edgy and restless, almost like he needed to bet again, to feel that shot of adrenalin he got when he had high stakes on the line. When he realized what it was, the thought sickened him.

While he was at the bus station he found a pamphlet that had been left by some Christian group and it explained, in simple terms how sin eats away at a person and ruins their true happiness. Kevin could see a pattern in what they were saying in this little pamphlet to what he had been watching lately on the religious station. It made a lot of sense but he had never been much for religion. From what he could figure out, Jesus was God's son and man was inherently sinful, imperfect. Basically, Jesus came to Earth to pay the sacrifice for man's sins, all they had to do was accept the free gift. Kevin was so unaware of all of this his whole life he hadn't even known that Eliza was a Catholic or what being a Catholic really meant. He bought the tickets and took a bus to the church she said she would meet him at.

"Hail Mary, full of grace, blessed art thou among women and blessed is the fruit of thy womb Jesus." Kevin heard Eliza reciting. He walked up and touched her shoulder. She jumped a bit, but when she looked up he realized that in some odd way, like the way an expensive skin cream makes a person look younger, Eliza's face was young-looking and sort of glowing. She was on her knees but he sat down next to her and let her go on. He looked around the church at the stained glass pictures of the crucifixion and the torture Jesus had gone through. Then he suddenly realized that when he was young his mother used to love watching "Jesus Christ Superstar" the musical when he was younger. These images brought back so many emotions, Kevin thought about the horrible direction his life had been taking and tried praying a little himself. He nearly started to sob as he did, thinking of his departed mom and his Dad that did little to really raise him when he died. Soon, mid-day mass started, and when the collection plate came around, it passed Kevin thousands of dollars richer. The pair left that day for Lethbridge with the weight of the world off their shoulders. Down there, Kevin found a treatment program that would help him with his addictions that he could take on a part-time basis, and both of them found jobs, simple ones that paid the bills and put food on the table. Two months later, they found out Eliza was pregnant and they realized that a child was in fact what was really missing from their lives, not money, not cars or diamond rings, just love, real love, true and unconditional. They also found this love in worshipping God and trying to live the way their creator had intended. Life was bliss for them, for the most part, from that point on.

SUNRISE

"And so class, I want you to look at pictures of different human forms and take a ruler and a pencil and try to make out the relationships of parts of a figure to others, for example, as I told you many times, eyes sit in a drawing at the halfway mark of a head and you draw around that dimension." As the art teacher said this, the final bell rang. "Okay, dismissed, everyone but Holly. Holly, I would like to see you for a few minutes after class." A din of moving books and bodies filled the aisles of the classroom and in seconds the class was emptied of all but Holly and her teacher.

Holly walked up to the teacher's desk and said, "Yes Mrs. Lange, what do you want to see me about?"

"Holly, I know you're going through some tough times, I have spoken to your mom, but I need to tell you Holly, the level of work you have been turning in won't get you any kind of scholarship, it may even get you kicked out of this school. The rules say you have to maintain a passing mark in your main class of your stream of choice. If you want to study art, you have to pass it."

"You don't understand Mrs. Lange." Holly said with a sigh. "After this weekend I'm being sent to my Dad's house in the Yukon and I'll be taking everything by correspondence. No more teachers, no more friends. No more art class." She said and dashed out the door. On her way out, she bumped into her friend Jeremy who had been observing the conversation. She really didn't want to talk to him at the moment but he followed her down the hall.

"Holly, you're moving away?" Jeremy asked. "Why didn't you tell me?"

"It's not permanent, and I didn't find out until yesterday." Holly said with a touch of anger in her voice. "Apparently I am stunting my mother's spiritual growth. Basically it means I'm getting in the way of her drinking and she wants to have her male friends sleep over. Not like she's hidden that from me anyways."

"Call me when you get in okay, we should talk about this." Jeremy said.

"Okay, I'll do that." Holly said, but she had no intention of calling him ever again. She didn't know what she was going to do, she loved her school, plus she was getting to be kind of popular with a lot of people. If only that zit-faced Jeremy would ease up a bit, things wouldn't be so bad. Or things wouldn't have been so bad she thought.

"Hey Holly." A voice came from behind her. She turned. It was Kurt. He was one of the best looking guys on the football team, was tall and muscular and she had only dreamed he would one day notice her.

"Oh hi Kurt, what's up?" Holly said.

"I was just kind of wondering how you were doing. Jen told me you were having troubles in your art class." He said.

"Oh, that's nothing. I just need to work harder. Well, actually, to be honest I am kind of down because I am being sent to my Dad's place up North and I don't really want to go."

"Are you serious? Are you going to miss the game on Sunday?"

"I'm not sure. I would like to go though." Holly said.

"Well, why don't you? After, maybe I can take you for MacDonald's and a movie. A little send-off thing."

"Hey, that would be cool." Holly hated MacDonald's. "Give me a call on my cell Saturday and if I can make it I would love to go." She said and scribbled down her number on a paper she had torn out of her binder.

"Great, hope to see you then." Kurt said and smiled. As he smiled at her, Holly felt like she was going to pass out from the thrill it gave her. For the rest of her day, she forgot about moving, forgot about art class, she was just beaming with joy.

The next day Holly woke up late and went downstairs to see how her mother was doing. She was laying on the couch with a broken martini glass on the floor beside her and the television was still on. The house was a mess, and even though in a few days she wouldn't be around to clean it again, she swept up the glass, vacuumed the rug, and put all the garbage in the kitchen pail and took it outside. Saturday mornings weren't something she was going to miss.

Later in the day Holly's mom got up and looked a hundred years old as she smoked a cigarette and lingered in the dining room over a coffee. Holly came down wanting to tell her about her date the next day but before she could, her mom said to her:

"What happened to my crystal martini glass Holly? Did you take it? Have you been drinking my gin?"

"No mom, I haven't been drinking any of your booze. You broke it while you were sleeping on the couch."

"I happen to remember very clearly putting my glass away dearie, and I don't appreciate the way you say things." Holly was taken aback, but she was used to this kind of treatment.

"I didn't drink any booze mom, I swear. Here, smell my breath." She said and leaned over towards her mom, who smacked her across the face.

"You're a horrible young girl Holly, I don't know how your father has agreed to put up with you. If it were me I would have turned you over to the government at birth!" Holly felt a gush of sadness and pain roll over her that squelched out the happiness she had felt the day before. She was speechless for a moment and then ran upstairs to her room. Her mom followed her up and closed off the door by propping a chair against it, then said, "that's where you'll stay until your father comes to get you, you rotten child!"

For a long time, Holly curled up in a ball and cried until she just felt numb about what had happened. She didn't know if she could ever forgive her mom for these sort of things, which had happened often. After concentrating her thoughts on the possibility of a Sunday date, she brought together her courage, used the 411 feature on her cell and got Kurt's home number. She dialed it and his younger sister answered. She asked for him and she screamed near the phone that he got a call and after a minute or so he finally got there.

"Hi, who's this?" Kurt said.

MUSTANG SUMMER   LEIF GREGERSEN

"Hi Kurt, this is Holly."

"Oh, hey—the pretty girl I took art class with last semester. How are you?"

"Not too bad... well, actually not that great. Are you good at climbing?"

Holly explained her situation and gave Kurt directions to her house and told him how to climb up the massive elm tree by her window and come in her room. In 40 minutes he was there, and she let him in undetected by her mom.

"Hey girl, what happened? You've got a bruise on your face." Kurt said once his breath had slowed from the climb.

"My mom hit me."

"Holy crap, why did she do that?"

"She thought I took her booze, but I didn't." Holly said.

"Speaking of booze, I have some on me. I thought you might want a sip or two." Kurt reached into his football team jacket and produced a mickey of cheap whiskey.

"I've never tried booze before, what does it do?"

"Never? Not even at Christmas for making toasts or anything?"

"Well, one time when I was eight my Dad let us have some Baby Duck Champagne and I took a gulp and my face went all red and I talked a lot. It was kind of weird. I got sick and never wanted to try it again." Holly said.

"Booze is funny. A little will make you relax, take the edge off of things, too much will make you sick. Here, have a sip, just a small one." Kurt said and offered forth the elixir. Holly took a small sip and had a bit of trouble swallowing, but got it down. It felt like it was on fire from her lips to her stomach.

"That's not too bad. I guess I could get used to it, but I would never want to end up like my mom." Holly said. "She drinks every day and ends up passing out.

"Man, that must suck. My parents are so religious they don't even keep any liquor. They give me enough allowance to put away a decent stash though. What's that like to have a mom who parties?"

"It's embarrassing, actually, especially when she has friends over. I never have friends over. By the way, just so you know, she locked me in here."

"Well then we'll just have to have our own party." He said and his broad smile made her wonder what was really on his mind. "So what's your dad like?" Kurt asked. "Does he treat you okay?"

"My Dad is the nicest guy in the world. He puts up with so much. I would normally want to live with him but where he lives now there's nothing, not even a town for 30 miles. He said he wanted to live like mankind was intended to. But I want to stay here and finish grade 12 so I can go to art school. Now I don't know what to do."

MUSTANG SUMMER   LEIF GREGERSEN

"I think I know what you can do." Kurt said.

"What?"

"Have another sip and let me kiss you." Kurt half expected Holly to slap him but she took the bottle from his hand, took a bigger sip than the first and pulled him towards her. She had never necked with anyone before, never known any guy as good looking as Kurt to see anything in her. To Holly, this was a magic carpet ride to another planet. She felt the pleasure ripples of the whiskey go through her and the sensuality of Kurt's kisses. The pair became like one, silently exploring each other's tongues and backs, and they went on for what seemed like hours. Kurt paused to drink more and then when they resumed he put his hand on her breast. She pulled it away and then they went on kissing. A few minutes later he got on top of her and she could feel his excitement but thought to herself finally that she didn't want to lose her virginity like this.

"Stop Kurt, I don't want to go that far." Holly said, breathless.

"Oh, come on, you know you want to do it." Kurt said.

"Kurt, get off me! Right now!" Holly raised her voice and then heard shouting from downstairs through her door.

"Holly, is that you?" Her mom shouted.

"Get off me. Now!" Holly said and heard her mom taking the chair from the door and opening it. Kurt pulled away from her just as Holly's mom burst in.

"Holly, what do you think you are doing? Under my roof?"

"It's okay mom, he was just leaving." Holly said and gave Kurt a dirty look.

"Young man, you are coming with me." Holly's mom said and grabbed Kurt by the arm and slammed her door shut, propped the chair against it and went downstairs. Holly waited. And waited. And waited. She thought for sure her mom was going to come back to punish her after she kicked Kurt out. Then finally, tired of waiting, she climbed out her window thinking her mom had passed out and Kurt had left, and when she got to the ground floor and looked in the kitchen window, there was Kurt—her dream man, naked and making love to her mother.

She knew how jocks were, they would all congratulate him and the word would spread like wildfire. Now she would be known as the girl whose mom puts out. Up until now she had thought that staying in Edmonton and finishing school was an option, albeit a remote one, but now she knew she could never face up to the other students after all of this.

Holly left the house, walked away, walked for a long time. She had her phone with her and called her dad's house. There was no answer. After she had been walking for miles, she saw what she felt then was her only way out—the famed High Level bridge. So many people killed themselves off of it there were fences built to keep them from jumping down to the roadway below. She walked out to the middle of the bridge, curled up and sat hidden behind a girder so no one would see her and call the police. She still felt the effects of

MUSTANG SUMMER   LEIF GREGERSEN

the whiskey in her head but it was fading. She had only one person to call, Jeremy.

"Hello? Holly?" He could see her number on his phone but at first she didn't say anything.

After a long pause, the words came, "Jeremy, do you know what it's like to really like someone and then see them with someone else?"

"Yeah, as a matter of fact, I know exactly how that feels." He said. "I heard about you having a date with that bonehead football star."

"I didn't think he was a bonehead. He worked hard in art class last year. He seemed nice."

"Jocks only work hard in the easy courses so they can get their average up and not get kicked off the team. That guy doesn't know how to love anybody." Jeremy said.

"And I suppose you do know how to love someone."

"Yes, I do. You respect them and you care for them and you get to know them and when they trust you, you take the next simple step. Guys like Kurt just want to get laid so they can brag to their friends."

"And you wouldn't brag to your friends if you got laid?"

"Aside from you Holly, I don't have any friends."

"I don't want to go to my Dad's Jeremy." Holly said, her sobs slightly audible.

"So stay here. What's the big deal?"

"I can't stay here either. Jeremy, I'm going to kill myself."

"Are you at home?"

"No, and don't call anyone. Just talk to me."

"Okay, just tell me what happened."

"Well, my mom got mad at me over nothing. Less than nothing. So she locked me in my room. Then I called Kurt and he came over with some whiskey…"

"You didn't…"

"I had some whiskey and we necked, but just listen."

"Okay, I'm sorry. Go on." Jeremy said.

"So we necked a bit and then he tried to make me have sex with him and I yelled and my mom heard me."

"I don't know if I want to listen to all of this."

"You probably don't. Let's just say that in the end Kurt and my mom ended up…"

"Oh my God Holly. I'm so sorry you had to go through that." Jeremy said, sounding concerned.

"It's over. I can't turn back time. But I have no way out and I think you're the only friend I still have. I'm so sorry Jeremy."

"Holly, you have nothing to be sorry about. I care about you. Oh, what the hell, I can say it, I love you. Now tell me where you are."

"Only if you won't call anyone. Come here yourself."

"Deal."

"I'm on the high level bridge."

In exactly 17 minutes Holly heard Jeremy yelling for her and she yelled back and he pulled his bike up to where she was on the bridge and got off beside where she was sitting.

"Holly, I've had a long time to think on my bike ride." He said as he sat down.

"You were here in two minutes. How is that a long time?"

"Well, I guess I have been planning this for a while. I made a contact in Banff and looked into what you need to get in to the school there and I think I found a spot for you at the Banff Centre For the Arts. I even found a job with the park service."

"But what about grade 12? We have three months to go."

MUSTANG SUMMER   LEIF GREGERSEN

"I have that all worked out. You can resume your art classes at the local school and together we can audit our other classes and just challenge the departmental." Jeremy said.

"But why are you doing this?" Holly said. "I hope you don't think I'm going to share a bed with you in return for you paying the rent."

"I'm going to live in the accommodations provided by the park service and you are going to live in a dorm. All I ask is that you take your art seriously, work hard and don't look back."

"But why would you do all this for me?" Holly said.

"Just to show you there are still good people in the world. I understand what you went through with your mom."

"How could you understand? No one could understand."

"I don't know why I never told you this, but the woman my dad is married to isn't my real mom."

"What?"

"My real mom moved away before I met you and my dad remarried. She took off and we never heard from her until a nurse in a hospital in Northern BC told us she had passed away. Never even got to say goodbye. She didn't booze it up so much, but she was abusive and ran around. It was horrible. But that's life. You take what they deal you and you play your hand as well as you can, even if you have to bluff all the time."

Holly put her arm around Jeremy and hugged him for a long time. She wept about growing up, about loss, about pain, and once she had cried all the tears she had to cry she looked out to the East and saw the sun rising. Summer was coming, and it was going to be a beautiful morning.

THE END

MUSTANG SUMMER   LEIF GREGERSEN

ON THE JOB

"So miss beautiful, I wanted to show you something I learned the other day." Ralph said as he looked in his girlfriend's brown shining eyes and let his gaze linger over her dark brown hair.

"Okay, what is it now? Another stupid joke?" Natalie said.

"No, just try it. Here, haven't you ever wondered why people have a 'ring finger' and why they put wedding and engagement rings on them?"

"Not really, but I'm sure you're going to tell me." She said.

"First, give me your hands. Now, take and touch all five fingers of your right hand to the fingers of your left hand and spread them out." Ralph said.

"This better not be some lame farmer's joke." Natalie said.

"No, this is cool. Okay, now take your middle fingers and touch the middle knuckles of them together so that when you look at your hands, together with the middle fingers and thumbs, you make a heart shape." She did so and smiled.

"Neat" She said.

"Okay, now in our lives we have four kinds of people we love. We start with our parents, symbolized by the two

144

MUSTANG SUMMER   LEIF GREGERSEN

touching index fingers. We love them, but we will leave them eventually, to have our own lives. Try to pull your index fingers apart and then put them back." Natalie did so and her index fingers came apart.

"Next, we have our brothers and sisters, symbolized by our pinkies. They are really important to us, and we love them to pieces, but eventually they will go have their own families, so we can separate from them." Natalie separated and wiggled her pinkies, and a look of intrigue came over her face.

"Okay," Ralph said, "next are our own children, that is what our thumbs symbolize. We teach them, they teach us, they love us and we love them, but eventually they will separate from us and go on to live their own lives. Separate your thumbs and put them back together." Ralph said. Natalie separated her thumbs and kept her fingers together and the heart shape with her middle fingers and thumbs.

"Now, finally, we have our true loves, our spouses. That is symbolized by two ring fingers. The love we have for our spouses never stops, we love them forever. Now try and separate from your spouse." Natalie's ring fingers didn't move as hard as she tried, for as long as she kept her other fingers together and formed the 'heart' shape with her middle fingers. She let out a laugh and said:

"Cool, I like that!" And then hugged Ralph and gave him a peck on the cheek.

"Okay, there's just one more part to it. Give me your right hand." Ralph said, and took something out of his pocket. He opened the small box, took a ring out of it and slid it onto

MUSTANG SUMMER LEIF GREGERSEN

her ring finger. "This is to show you how much I want to keep you in my life forever."

"Oh, Ralphie! It's beautiful!" Natalie said with joy, and leaned in to kiss him. "Does this mean we're engaged?"

"Well, for now, let's call it a promissory ring. It just means I love you sweetie." Ralph said. "But I'm sorry, I'm running a bit late. I have to go in to work now."

"Can't you call in sick? I know you hate that job anyway. Wouldn't you rather be with me?" Natalie said with a mischievous look on her face.

"I wish I could, but I need the cash and we've got a whole weekend together in just two more days."

"Call me on your break okay."

"I will sweetheart, I promise. But I really have to go." Ralph picked up his security guard officer's hat, zipped up his jacket and headed out the door, blowing a kiss to Natalie as he closed it. Ralph paused for a moment outside her door and thought about how much he wanted to stay. But he walked out to the street, got in his sub-compact light green Nissan, started the engine and drove off towards downtown.

Ralph's job was starting to eat away at him, working the night shift at an all-night drug store in downtown Edmonton. He had to drink so much coffee and pop all night to keep himself alert all night. Doing this made him even more nervous than he already was from having to be the authority figure in public. He hated confronting people,

146

couldn't stand having to deal with anyone and everyone who walked in the door of the drug store.

Ralph turned the radio up louder than he should on the classic rock station and tapped the steering wheel as he speeded off to work from Natalie's 124 street apartment building. In only 20 minutes, he was pulling in behind the store he was to guard and he shut down his car and went in to relieve the guard that had been working the shift before him.

"Hey Stan, how did things go?" Ralph asked the other security guard

"Oh, same old same old. Some drunk teenagers kicked over the newspaper boxes, a couple people got verbally abusive when I told them we don't have a public bathroom. I'll never understand some of these people. They think if they get angry enough, I'll somehow let them use our bathroom, like I'm lying to them or something. To tell you the truth, it kind of amuses me a bit that these drunken jerks are going to head out of here and wet themselves. I suppose most of them just go and urinate around back anyway though." Stan said with a confident laugh.

"Well, if you like, you can take off now. Are you back here tomorrow morning?"

"Yeah, I'll be here at 0800, for sure." Stan said.

"Grab me a Tim Horton's coffee if you get the chance, extra large double double." Ralph said.

"Will do my friend, have a good night." Stan reached out his hand to seal the deal and Ralph took it and shook it firmly. "By the way, cheques are out tonight, so watch it when it gets to be around 0200. Things might get a little nuts."

"Thanks Bud, take care." Cheques are out! Damn, Ralph thought to himself. He had forgotten. Maybe he should have called in sick. Around the end of every month, all the pension and disability and welfare cheques were direct deposited to people's accounts right at 0200. Most of the people that got these cheques would call their bank and then head for the nearest ATM. Soon after all the emergency rooms and hole in the wall bars were full until the money was spent. A lot of people called that particular day of the month Mardi Gras, which stood for fat Tuesday. At some point during or after these events, a lot of those people ended up here, at the only all night drug store downtown. Tonight was going to be nuts!

Ralph started out his shift pacing around the store, and after an hour not much had happened. Then a group of twenty-somethings came in and lingered around for a while. They didn't seem to be doing much or buying anything, so Ralph kept a close eye on them. A couple of them separated from the group and were reading magazines. Even though he hated being the one to do it, he told them they had to buy the magazines before they read them. The pair gave him a dirty look and put the magazines back then they went outside with their friends and smoked for a while in front of the store. One of them came back in and walked right up to Ralph and said,

"Why the hell you giving my friends a hard time?" He was a short guy, which was something Ralph had been told to be cautious of, short guys always seemed to have something to prove. The dude stepped in closer, almost challenging him and Ralph reacted by sticking out his arm straight, putting it

MUSTANG SUMMER   LEIF GREGERSEN

right against the guy's chin and then cocking his other arm back. He figured if he kept this guy at arm's length he wouldn't have a chance to get the first punch in. But he didn't like the look of the guy. He had stone cold eyes like he had some training and likely some experience in fighting. Adrenalin shot through his mind and body and he yelled,

"Get the F*&K away from me!"

"Why what are you going to do?" The short guy said.

"I'm going to defend myself is what I'm going to do." Ralph said, his voice and body shaking.

"Are you some kind of woosy? Who the hell sticks his fist out like that?" Ralph didn't take his arm down.

"Get the hell out of my store, now!" Ralph said in a commanding tone.

"I'm not going to leave, I'm going to shop." He said.

"No, you're going to leave. Now!" Ralph looked over at the seemingly disinterested cashier. "Call the police!" He said to her.

The cashier picked up the phone and called the police, but then hung up right away and said they put her on hold. Ralph felt like he wanted to scream at her for not doing anything, but then two of the short guy's friends came in.

"Get him out of here." The cashier said to them and they each grabbed an arm and pulled him out. Ralph was visibly shaken by the whole thing, all he could think about

MUSTANG SUMMER   LEIF GREGERSEN

was how much he hated this job and that it made him take risks like he did just now. It was the same old story that had gone on with him since junior high, some guy wanted to prove himself and maybe because Ralph was taller or better looking, or even just the closest person on hand they picked on him, maybe hoping by knocking him down a peg or two they could boost their own image.

Ralph had hoped the incidences of this phenomenon would lessen when he got older but for some reason it didn't. In fact in many ways it had gotten worse. The hardest part of it was that when he was a teenager he had dropped out of school because of it and now, without an education, all he could get was jobs where bullies like this thrived. There was one at the car wash he had worked at last year, pushing people around and screaming at them all with full support of the owner, there were people like that at the plastics plant he worked in, a job that he got through a temp agency that he still worked through now and then when he needed extra money. Even the staff at the temp agency office liked to push people around a lot. Sometimes he thought that if it weren't for Natalie there would just be no point in living his life.

Ralph bought himself a bottle of diet soda hoping to sooth his worn nerves and paced around more, wondering what the rest of the night was going to be like. 0200 came around and the poor and unwanted started to trickle in. It was sad really, a lot of these people had serious problems and it definitely seemed that they didn't get enough money because he would only see them for the first few days of the month. A lot of them stocked up on cigarettes, some of them would buy tea and sugar and others would blow everything on all the expensive grocery items the drug store stocked.

Finally at around 0430 things slowed down and Ralph went in the back for his break.

Ralph ate a sandwich Natalie had made for him and was drinking another diet soda and then called her up to tell her how delicious the food had been and how much he wished he had taken her suggestion. They talked for a few minutes and then Ralph wanted to get a magazine he had been reading from his car and he went out to the main part of the store. To his great surprise, there was a guy with a mask on waving a knife around and screaming at one of the cashiers, telling her to open the till and give him all the cash. Ralph stopped dead in his tracks and backed into the back room.

"Natalie, call the cops, tell them the store is being robbed!"

"Okay, stay on the line with me, I'll three-way call them." Natalie called 911 on the other line and was back in a few seconds, the three people linked together.

"Who am I talking to?" The 911 dispatcher asked.

"I'm Ralph, I'm the security guard here at the 24 hour Drug Mart on 121st and Jasper."

"Are you armed?"

"I have a collapsible night stick but I've never used it before."

"Ralph, listen to me, that guy could be crazy, you have to go out there and protect the cashiers. We have help on the way but it could be a few minutes. Who all is there?"

151

MUSTANG SUMMER   LEIF GREGERSEN

"There is just me and two cashiers. The pharmacist is off tonight." Ralph said. "I don't know if I can do this, I don't have any training."

"Ralphie, you have to help them." Natalie said in an upset voice. A wave of fear went through Ralph's body when Natalie said this but somehow he felt more able to control it. Just knowing Natalie cared so much for him and was behind him always made him feel stronger. He put the phone on speaker, put it in his pocket, then took out his nightstick and, with a flick of the wrist, it opened to it's full, menacing 3 foot length.

"Okay, I'm going out there." Ralph said toward his pocket. He opened the door and walked at a quick pace towards the front and yelled, "Drop the knife, right now!"

"Up yours!" The man said and took a step toward Ralph. If nothing else, he was distracting the guy from harming either of the cashiers. As the guy got close, Ralph responded in a flash, smacking the guy's wrist, making the knife drop from his hand. The guy just looked even angrier than he was, he had some kind of scary look in his eye. He reached into his pocket and took a small pistol out. Ralph froze for a moment and the guy pointed it at him. He closed his eyes, waiting for the gunshot that would end his life but somewhere off in the distance the sound of sirens was coming closer. The robber hesitated, and turned around and ran out of the store and jumped into a car that was parked right by the entrance.

Ralph ran out and tried to read the license plate number and get a good look at the car, but the driver had his

152

lights off and sped off before Ralph could read the plate. The best he could do was make a mental note that it was a red, early 80's Ford coupe. His heart was pounding but he ran to his car, fumbled with the keys for a second, then opened the door, got in and had it in gear a split second after he finished starting it. He pulled out of the lot, then sped west on Jasper Avenue as fast as his little engine could take him. He saw nothing, then trolled around the area looking for any sign of where the car may be. By chance, Ralph, in his heightened state of mind, spotted the car parked in the driveway of a high-rise apartment building. He pulled in behind it and told the 911 dispatcher the license number and location of the car. He was about to back away and leave the possibly deadly situation but a delivery van all of a sudden pulled in behind him. He got out of his car and started waving at the van to back out and then the man who had just tried to shoot him came out of the car.

Ralph panicked and jumped back into his Nissan, put the car in gear and slammed into the car in front of him, then backed up just as quickly and slammed into the van. In his rush, Ralph stalled the engine, and before he could get it started again the robber was at his window, pointing his pistol at Ralph.

"Oh my freaking God!" Ralph said, loud enough for the dispatcher and Natalie to hear him. Instinctively, he reached for the door handle and opened it carefully, not letting the bandit see what he was doing. Then, just as it seemed like once again the suspect was going to pull the trigger, Ralph whipped the door open, slamming it into him. It knocked the gun out of his hand and then Ralph got out and got angry.

MUSTANG SUMMER   LEIF GREGERSEN

"Do you have any freaking idea who you're messing with?" Ralph said. He punched the criminal in the face and he went down, then he wrestled him onto his front and handcuffed him. When the police got there all they had to do was load the guy into their patrol car. Then he called his supervisor who told him not to talk to the press and sent down two security patrol car drivers to deal with the situation.

Two days later, the local newspaper ran a story about the robbery. Apparently the guy who had tried to pull it off had done a few bad deeds before. He had done enough to be listed as a dangerous offender and at the time was known to, and somewhat feared by, the city police and was also on the run from a warrant for assault causing bodily harm. That night he got a call from his boss and then before he could call Natalie the phone rang again.

"Hello?" Ralph said, answering the phone on the second ring.

"You have a phone call from," The voice paused, then changed tone and said, "'Edmonton Remand Centre.' To accept the charges, please press one. To decline, press two." Ralph wasn't sure what to do, but he pressed the number one to accept the call. His stomach tightened as he waited for someone to threaten him from the jail.

"Hello? Ralph?" This is Jason, remember—Jason Bunter from school."

"Yeah, man, what's up?" Ralph was really reluctant to talk any further, he couldn't see any good coming of this.

154

Jason had been one of his bullies from school, in fact the one that had been the reason he had dropped out of school.

"I just wanted to say man that it has been eating away at me for quite some time the way I used to treat you. I really treated you like crap in school and I'm sorry. I read the article about what you did, that took some guts. I never had any guts man, I just picked on people who were smaller than me and I ended up messing up my life because I never was anybody. I just wanted you to know that."

"But why me? Why are you telling me this now?"

"I had something happen man, I became a Dad and I decided I had to own up to my life. I pulled a couple of scams and turned myself in. I read about you in the paper and just wanted to own up to you as well."

"Thanks man, that means a lot to me."

"Yeah, congrats again man, that guy is in here now and no one likes him anyway. And don't worry, he won't get out again. I heard from a guard they got video of him and with his record he won't see the light of day for a lot of years."

"Cool, I appreciate you letting me know Jason."

Ralph hung up and felt a happy feeling go through him for the first time in a long time. He picked up the phone again and called Natalie.

"Hey babe. You won't believe what just happened to me."

"I don't know if you will believe my news either."

"What's up?" Ralph said.

"You first." Natalie said.

"Well, a guy who used to bully me called up and said some really nice things. Makes me feel pretty good. I don't feel so bad now being just a security guard."

"Ralphie, I always knew you were more than just a security guard. You're a great human being, I picked you for a reason."

"That's pretty sweet. By the way, before that guy called, my boss called as well and he said he's going to get me off regular guard work now. He wants me to stay with the company, says my name and skills are important to his business. He wants me up in the office now as the scheduler. I'll have my own office and everything. And a good deal more money."

"Well, that makes my news even better news."

"Come on, quit with the suspense." Ralph said.

"You remember that night when you came home from working out of town for a week and I came over and we..."

"What is it?"

"First I want to ask if you really want to marry me?"

MUSTANG SUMMER   LEIF GREGERSEN

"Of course, I just wasn't 100% sure yet because of my crappy job. It was practically minimum wage, it took me six months just to save up for that tiny ring."

"Well, lets just say we're going to need the extra income and we better get married within the next 9 months." Ralph grinned from ear to ear.

"You mean?"

"I mean."

"You rock babe. You are my world."

"No Ralphie, you're the one that's awesome. By the way, I hope this new job lets you come home every night because I got a great idea. You remember telling me how good you did in accounting in school before you dropped out?"

"Yeah, why?"

"Well, my Dad likes you and he gave me a great idea and wants to help out. He said he would pay for you to take a home study accounting course. It would take a while, but it would mean a lot for our future, if you want to do it. Accountants make good money and get a lot of respect."

"I don't think I've ever been more ready. Tell the soon to be grampa I'll do it."

"I already did."

"I love you Natalie. I'm going to make you proud."

"You already did."

ALL THE LITTLE PEOPLE

"So anyways man, are you in?" Stew asked his buddy Dean over the phone.

"Not if I have to drive man. I'm always the designated drinker and you're always the designated driver." Dean said.

"Why do I always have to drive dude? Can't you get your Dad's car? You have a license."

"I'm not on his insurance. Nobody under 25 remember." Dean said.

"Why don't you drive my car then?" Stew asked.

"Yeah, and let your mom see me when I pull in and you're all liquored up? Forget it."

"Alright, alright. Anyways, I have some good news for you. Jessica is going to be at the bush bash tonight." Stew said.

"Jessica? My dream girl? How do you know for sure?"

"Her best friend told me. I just called her up."

"Man, I will never understand how every red hot babe teams up with girls no guy wants to be around." Dean said.

"Guys do it too. Look at you and me."

"Yeah, I am pretty kind to let you hang out with me."

"Actually I meant it the other way. But anyhow, be ready at six with the beer, I'll get my mom's car as soon as she gets home."

"You got it bro. See you then, later." Dean said and hung up the phone.

"Dean, what the hell is this? You're going drinking again?" Dean's father said, from behind him, making Dean cringe.

"Dad, don't sneak up on me like that. Yeah, I'm going to have a couple of beers."

"How many beers do you plan to take with you?"

"I bought a 24 pack. I'll be lucky to drink six, you know how these parties go."

"Well, you can leave your old man six of them for starters. I don't feel like making another trip out tonight."

"Sure, no problem Dad." Dean went into the fridge and pulled out six cans of beer and handed them over. Silently, under his breath, he said the word: "Lush."

"What the hell did you just say?" Dean's dad shouted.

"Nothing, here, take your beer." Dean said and handed over the precious cans. "I might stay out all night, we're going out to the gravel pits off Villeneuve Road."

"Holy crap, kids still party there? Did I ever tell you that's where I met your mother?"

"A hundred times Dad. If that's all I have to get a shower in before Stew gets here."

"All right, all right. Go, don't let me stop you." Dean's dad said.

Dean hopped in the shower, put the water on cold at first and felt it shock his skin from head to toe. Then he started to think about his dad and all the shit he had been going through and just stood in the icy water, banging his head against the wall of the shower for two minutes. Then he opened his eyes and took a deep breath and tried to clear up his thoughts. He turned the hot water on and took a long relaxing shower then stepped out of the shower and shaved, even though he didn't need it, and put on some aftershave and sprayed on some body spray then brushed his teeth. Then he got dressed and walked out to check the window to see if Stew had come yet. His Dad was already on his third beer and was lying on the couch seemingly asleep with the TV off.

"You smell like some kind of fruit Dean." His dad said without moving.

"Thanks for the vote of confidence dad." Dean said.

"You know women don't want you to be all fashionable like that. When I met your mother I had been in a fight and had blood all over my shirt. Women like real men, the ones that will fight and stand up for them.

"Okay dad, I'll keep that in mind." Dean went back to his room and sorted through the CD's he wanted to take to play in Stew's car. After about ten minutes, he heard honking coming from out the balcony window and he looked out to see that it was Stew. Dean got his three remaining six-packs and rushed out the door. After it closed, he said,

"See ya, wouldn't want to be ya." He muttered under his breath. Suddenly, he heard a shoe thump on the inside of the door. How the hell could he have heard that? Dean thought.

The September sun was waning in the sky as the pair raced down Villeneuve Road to their destination. They were headed for what everyone called 'the pits' which was a massive yard owned by a St.Albert road construction company. No one ever seemed to mind people partying in there and it was a good ways from anyone who might complain, so it had remained a party spot for generations.

On this Friday night one of the people attending the party happened to be the son of the owner of a car dealership and he had somehow gotten the keys for five 4X4 trucks to lend to his friends. They were spinning out, sloshing through massive puddles, and running their trucks up steep inclines. It was chaos, but it was really good clean fun, provided the dealership owner didn't discover what his son was doing. Stew parked his mom's car some distance away from where the 4X4's were and they took out their beer and walked up to join the rest of the teenagers that were there.

Soon after they got there, Dean saw Jessica and some girl next to her that he didn't know. He really wanted to talk to his 'dream girl' so he downed a few beers as quick as he

MUSTANG SUMMER   LEIF GREGERSEN

could to try and build up a bit of liquid courage. Then he walked right up to her and said hi. At first she gave him a bit of a dirty look, but before she could say anything he said:

"Jessica, you have to introduce me to your friend. Hi, I'm Dean. Jessica and I go to high school together."

"I'm Amanda. Pleased to meet you." She said and put out her hand for him to squeeze.

"Where you from Amanda?"

"I live on a farm about 20 km north of here. I go to Sturgeon Composite."

"Cool. What you do for fun out there?"

"Mostly try to meet handsome boys like you." She said, making Dean grin a mile wide.

"Amanda, I think I'm going to go say hi to Travis. Are you okay to stay here by yourself?" Jessica said.

"Yeah, that's fine, go ahead." Amanda said. Already Dean's head was full of this new girl and he didn't care much that Jessica was obviously slighting him.

"Can I buy you a drink?" Dean said and handed her a beer.

"Yeah, that's cool of you. Thanks."

Dean and Amanda talked on for the next while about people they knew that went to each other's schools. Dean was

163

MUSTANG SUMMER   LEIF GREGERSEN

kind of surprised that Amanda had to go to church; he had barely seen the inside of one since he was 14. He liked going to church even though he often was too hung over to attend. Things had gone weird in the past couple of years. He told her about how it had been kind of a rough transition for him to attend high school and Amanda seemed to intuitively know what he meant. Before they knew it, the sun was going down and some people had made a fire and put some logs out for partygoers to sit on.

The two youngsters sat down and sipped at more beers and watched the flames lapping in the darkness and then all of a sudden a shooting star fell. Dean asked her if she saw it and she said she did and then he asked her what wish she had made. She said "This one." And leaned in to kiss him. Dean kissed back and they kissed passionately for some time. After they were necking for almost 20 minutes they paused for air and Stew came up and asked for the rest of the beer. There were seven cans left and Dean handed them over. Then he asked Amanda if she wanted to go for a walk and she said it was okay.

They walked for a while and looked up at the sky and the billion stars that came out in these dark places away from city lights like the Villeneuve pits and it seemed so easy and refreshing just to talk and walk. Dean kind of wanted to but he didn't make any further moves on Jessica. Somehow he knew she felt the same way.

"So are you going to be okay to drive home then?" Amanda asked.

"Oh, I don't drive. I gave it up." Dean said, feeling comfortable for the first time in forever talking about it.

"Why? What happened?"

"Well, one night my dad was drinking at a party out of town he took me to, and I had my license so he got me to drive him home. He was in a good mood. As we went down the highway he kept telling me to drive faster and faster, and I kind of liked it. His old car was awesome, a Dodge Charger. We were flying down the highway and suddenly there was a deer on the road and we hit it and the car flipped. I wound up in the hospital needing stitches and a pin in my bone in this arm." He patted his left arm as he said this. "They said I had a bad concussion so they kept me there. The worst thing about it was that at the time my mom was sick, she had been diagnosed with pancreatic cancer and it had gone into stage four. It was over in a moment, despite all her pain. She just went. Passed away just like a whisper my Dad said. I keep thinking it was my fault, keep thinking I could have done something differently to keep her alive Not to mention that I was tormented with the thought that I could have so easily killed my Dad right then too. I swore I would never drive again. "

"I'm sorry." Amanda said.

"It's just the way things are. Just who I am." Amanda went quiet and so did Dean and they just walked until they got near the party again.

On their way back they saw police cars on the highway, three of them, stopped and looking at the fire the partiers had made. They had the sense not to come into the crowd, they waited out on the highway until it dissipated. Everyone went into a controlled panic thinking they were going to get

MUSTANG SUMMER   LEIF GREGERSEN

arrested for underage drinking or trespassing and they all headed back to their cars and trucks. Dean saw Stew getting into his car way off and asked Amanda to stay where she was and wait for him, and told her he would be back right away. He ran up and Stew was just about to pull out.

"Dude, what are you doing? How many of those beers did you have?" Dean asked as Stew started up his mom's car.

"Just a few man, I'm okay. All I have to do is drive the car out of the pits, and then the cops can't touch me. I won't be trespassing and I'm not that drunk. I had maybe nine beers over five hours." Stew said.

"Just take it easy okay! They can still bust you for drinking and driving with that much booze in you. Go park on that range road off to the right and I'll meet you. I have to get this Amanda chick's phone number."

"Cool man, good work by the way bro." Stew reached out and fist-bumped Dean. "See you in a few minutes then."

Dean rushed back to where Amanda was and she had gone. He ran over to where some of the people were left and couldn't find her. Finally, feeling like crap, he walked the mile and a half up the highway to where Stew was waiting.

"Did you get her number?" Was all he said.

"No man, no I didn't get her number. Let's just get out of here."

Stew swung the car around and went into the ditch a little farther than he should have while making the turn. Dean

MUSTANG SUMMER   LEIF GREGERSEN

noticed but said nothing, then as they went further down the highway Stew nodded a couple of times and the car started to weave.

"Stop this car!"

"Whu... what? What's going on?" Stew said.

"You're drunk Stew. Or just stupid. Stop the car already.

"Okay, okay. You can drive then." Stew pulled the car over to the side of the highway.

"I don't drive!" Dean yelled.

"So what are we going to do then? What is your bright idea?"

"My bright idea is that I shouldn't even associate with people like you in the first place." Dean got out of the car and slammed the door shut. Stew drove up beside him and opened the window.

"Dean man, don't be a jerk. Come on, it's ten miles to St. Albert. Get back in already." Dean responded by giving Stew the finger, and Stew yelled, "Fine!" and drove off.

All Dean had on his mind was Amanda as he walked the long miles in darkness home. She was so kind and sweet. She was just like him, only a more gentle and caring kind of person. He wondered if he really was in love. Then he realized that in the hours since he had met her he hadn't even thought about Jessica. That had to mean something.

167

It took nearly three hours to get home and when he got there, Dean's dad was passed out on the couch with six empty beer cans beside him. His legs were so sore and he was so tired it didn't even faze him; he just went into his room and flopped on the bed. He was asleep in minutes.

A few short hours later, the sun woke Dean up and he pulled out his cell phone and called Stew's number. No answer. He tried again several times, he felt really bad about what he had done and said, and wanted to let his best friend know it was all because of the girl he had met and that he was ticked off he hadn't found out her last name or phone number or anything.

Dean drifted back to sleep and when he woke up later that morning he had expected to see a message on his phone from Stew, but there wasn't one. He started wondering why this might be, and decided to phone Stew's mom. She answered and told Dean that Stew hadn't come home. Now he really knew something was amiss. He took his bike out of their storage closet and carried it downstairs and started biking off to where Stew's house was. From there he would follow the route to the Villeneuve pits and if anything had gone wrong, maybe he could help.

Dean got all the way to the pits and saw nothing. He was starting to feel pretty exhausted, the long walk, and the long bike ride. But he was on a mission. He had to find his buddy.

On the way back Dean took a different route just in case Stew had missed a certain turnoff to where his house was and his gambit paid off. He almost wished it hadn't, he

MUSTANG SUMMER   LEIF GREGERSEN

wasn't prepared for what he found. Stew's car had slid off the road, flipped, maybe a few times, and was now teetering on its side. Inside the car, Stew was unconscious and blood was flowing from somewhere. Dean couldn't get inside to help him so he pushed with everything he had and somehow managed to tip the small car back onto its wheels with a hard slam.

The first thing Dean did was check for breathing. Good, he's still breathing, Dean thought. Then he checked pulse. Slow. Weak. That was bad, but better than stopped. He tried to pull Stew out of the vehicle and when he turned the young man's head, he saw that he was bleeding out of his ear. That was very bad. Stew had to get to a hospital. And fast. The first thing Dean did was put Stew in the back seat of the car and then he got behind the wheel, and by some miracle the thing started. He slid it into gear and cautiously pulled out. It was a bumpy ride, but he got the car back on the road. Dean accelerated the car up to highway speed and then all of a sudden he got a flashback of his mom, an image of her kind face and all he could think about was smashing into something, making his mother die of a broken heart. He shook off the feeling and kept on driving. It took everything he had just to keep the car between the white lines.

Dean slowed down to less than the speed limit and nearly stopped the car and then from behind him he heard Stew let out a moan. I can't fail him now, Dean thought to himself, and stepped hard on the gas. After another agonizing ten minute drive, Dean pulled into the emergency driveway of the Sturgeon Hospital. He ran in and half yelled, half screamed for help and though they seemed annoyed at first, when the hospital staff saw the blood on his shirt, they rushed out to see what had happened. The St. Albert Doctors did all

MUSTANG SUMMER   LEIF GREGERSEN

they could, and then had him airlifted to the University Hospital for emergency neurosurgery. Dean spent the next agonizing six hours in the waiting room with Stew's mom waiting to hear whether Stew was going to make it.

Finally, a surgeon came out and pulled off his mask, and when Stew's mom saw him force a smile she burst into tears of joy. Dean found it hard to keep from crying, especially when the Doctor shook his hand and told him he was a hero.

The next Monday Dean went back to school. A lot of people asked about what had happened, what he had done, how was Stew doing. It felt good for the first little while, but Dean soon got tired of the attention. Finally, at the end of lunch he managed to corner Jessica.

"Jessica, I don't suppose you have Amanda's number do you?"

"I'm sorry, I don't. I don't know her that well, I just met her that night. From what I understand she doesn't go to parties much."

"Well, if you see her again," Dean tore off a piece of paper and wrote his number on it. "Can you give her this?"

"Yeah, sure, but it may be a while."

"Whenever you can." Dean said.

Stew was eventually transferred back to the hospital in St. Albert where they wanted to keep him for a couple of weeks and Dean tried to visit him every day. The two of them swore they would talk to someone about their drinking and commiserated as Dean told Stew how much he wanted to see Amanda again. One day Dean's school was closed for maintenance issues and he went to see Stew early. He was being released that day and the pair went in his mom's new car back to his house and hung out for a while. Dean went home early that day, just after 1:00pm and his Dad had come home and had fallen asleep on the couch. His car keys were sitting next to him and Dean decided that it was time for things to change in his life. He took the keys, drove all the way to Sturgeon Composite High School with a bunch of daisies he had picked himself, and found Amanda sitting alone in the lunch room, and he saw her face light up when he came into sight. Everything was going to be okay from now on Dean thought.

MUSTANG SUMMER   LEIF GREGERSEN

GOING BACK

It had been a long, hot summer, and most of it was spent outdoors, pumping gas, driving his car, playing video games, or drinking beer. But at the end of it when September started to loom closer, Terry was left with the idea that he was slipping away from the anchors that had made his life fun up until now. He still hadn't had a steady girlfriend, he still hadn't gone all the way. He had been to parties and made some friends, but when September rolled around, all the people his age would be in University or High School, and in a way that terrified him. There was a vast expanse of options, a whole world of freedom left open for him, but he feared that freedom the same way a bungy jumper fears leaving the safety of the platform. There may be a whole lot of fun to be had, but if you don't jump off you don't have to risk anything. Not to mention that every relationship he had been in up until now was a disaster and the only way he knew how to meet decent girls was in school. So, despite that he had already graduated that Spring, Terry signed up to take a couple of classes at his old High School since it was already too late to apply for University.

It didn't take Terry long to pick out the girl he wanted to pursue above all the others. In fact, he was sitting in a grade 10 Law class on the very first day and she walked in. He figured she had to be the one. She had everything. Beautiful eyes, beautiful hair. She was even wearing shorts that revealed shapely legs with a nice tan on them. Terry soon learned that her name was Sonya, and that she had just moved into town. It wasn't a surprise that Terry had picked her out. The surprise was that when she walked into class she

MUSTANG SUMMER   LEIF GREGERSEN

looked in his eyes and smiled at him and walked right up and sat down in the desk in the back row next to him. The only problem was that Terry found it nearly impossible to speak to her, as he did to most women. He was struck dumb by the vast expanse of that unknown territory that had separated boys from girls from his very first day of school 13 years before.

"I'm telling you man, she's into me. She looks at me, she says hi every day and smiles." Terry said into the phone.

"It's been three weeks since school started and you come up with this now? Why don't you call her then?" His best friend Tony said.

"I'm kind of nervous."

"So sit down right now and have a couple of drinks and then call her up."

"You know, that's not a bad idea." Terry said.

"Of course it isn't. You can't let time wait on this. Women don't stay single for long. Especially if she looks as good as you say she does."

"You're right man, I'm going to do it. I'll let you know how it goes." Terry hung up the phone and went to get one of his Dad's beer. He guzzled it and then grabbed another. He felt sick, but sipped at the second beer anyway and got the phone book. There it was, Tucker, Larry. 52 Lancaster Crescent, 555-1646. He picked up the phone, but held the plunger down, then downed the last of his second beer, waited for a wave of nausea to pass and dialed the number.

"Hello?"

"Hi, is this Sonya?"

"Yes, it is, who is calling?"

"This is Terry. I sit next to you in Law Class. I was just kind of wondering. Um... Uhhh..."

"Are you calling to ask me out?" She said, sounding like he had paid her a compliment.

"Yeah, I guess so. I wanted to see if you would go to the fall dance with me."

"I would have loved to Terry, that's very sweet of you, but I'm seeing somebody."

"Who are you seeing?"

"Brock."

"Brock the jock? That guy who's always saying he's going to play in the NFL?"

"Yeah, that's him." Sonya said.

"Oh, sorry, I didn't know. Hey-see you in class tomorrow, okay?"

"Sure, sounds good Terry. Thanks for asking." Terry heard a click and he wasn't sure if it was a heart valve bursting or the phone disconnecting. He sat in his chair for a

MUSTANG SUMMER   LEIF GREGERSEN

long time, then went up to his bedroom and laid flat on his back, staring up at the ceiling for a long time.

In a few days Terry started to feel better but he dropped Law class. He felt incredibly foolish and didn't want to have to keep thinking about Sonya. He figured that he wouldn't need to be a Lawyer if he just went off and joined the French Foreign Legion when Brock found out he had tried to ask Sonya out. It had to be safer than facing down that giant. The day of the fall dance his buddy Tony called up.

"Hey man, how you feeling?" Tony asked.

"I'm surviving. You going to that dance?" Terry asked.

"Nah, I don't think so. I got a movie lined up, Jackie Chan. Want to come over and watch it?"

"I could see my way to doing that. What you got for refreshments?"

"Mickey of bourbon and 12 pack of beer."

"In that case I'm there." Within 12 minutes Terry was knocking at Tony's door.

"Come in dude, make yourself at home." Tony said as he opened the door, brandishing a cold beer for Terry.

"Let's start off with a couple of shots." Terry said, eager to forget that Brock and Sonya would be in each other's arms that night. Tony got the shot glasses and poured them each one.

"Here's to friendships, old and new." And both of them downed their first shot.

"You know Tony, I think that I could have been good friends with Sonya. She's the kind of girl that respects people, doesn't use their vulnerabilities to hurt them. You remember that rich chick I went out with a couple of times back in grade eleven? She wouldn't even go near an arcade like it was some kind of opium den." Tony filled both shot glasses a second time and took his shot in hand.

"And here's to forgetting some friendships."

"Did I ever tell you how Sonya's eyes were this amazing red brownish color. Like no eyes I've ever seen."

"And here's to shutting up about something your friend is tired of hearing about."

"Sorry man, I just can't believe she would end up with that overstuffed, steroid using jerk. I should have taken your advice earlier."

"Listen bro, have a beer, take a long breath and then I think you and I should walk over to the dance. I'll run interference and you talk to Sonya. I think you might be surprised at what she has to say to you."

"Are you serious? What do you know? What did you hear?"

"I don't know a whole lot, but I heard something about the pair of them having a one-way relationship. Namely, she is looking to get out of the whole thing."

MUSTANG SUMMER   LEIF GREGERSEN

"Man, I love you!" Terry said and put his arm around Tony's shoulder and shook him.

"Save it for the ladies dude."

The pair drank another beer and took another one with them and walked the 15 or 20 blocks to the High School where the dance was being held. When Tony and Terry got there, Terry noticed right away that Sonya wasn't pleased with the way things were going. She was sitting at a table with no one else at it and Brock was off dancing with another girl. Tony told Terry to go talk to her and that he would keep watch in case anything happened. Terry walked up and sat down next to Sonya.

"Hey Sonya. How come you aren't dancing?"

"Oh hey Terry. Brock doesn't like it when I dance with other guys."

"But he's over there dancing with a girl."

"I know. I'm getting pretty sick of him. Don't tell anyone but I think we are going to break up."

"Oh, sorry to hear that." Terry lied.

"Yeah, I should have known he would be the jealous, crazy type. He seemed like such a nice guy before. I met him last year before he got into the whole football thing. I was staying here with my cousin and she liked him too. I kind of suspect he's taking steroids so I think I have to end it. He is crazy jealous and always threatens people." Just as she said this, Terry felt his shoulder being pulled at.

"Hey goof boy. What do you think you're doing talking to my girl?"

"Oh, sorry man. We were just talking."

"Well now you're done talking. Blow." Brock said.

"Don't be such a jerk Brock. This is exactly what I told you I don't want you doing. This guy is my friend, we're in Law 10 together."

"Listen bitch, I don't care if he's your brother. When you're out with me, you're out with me."

"Hey relax, Sonya didn't do anything. And I said I'm sorry. I'll leave now."

"And I think I'm leaving too." Sonya said.

"Stay where you are!" Brock said to Sonya. Terry stood up and Brock punched him in the stomach, knocking the wind out of him.

"Leave him alone Brock. If you want me to stay that bad I'll stay." Terry was doubled over and couldn't say anything. Brock gave him a hard shove and he stumbled off, hearing the pair argue as he left. Tony came and helped him out the door.

"Geez man, what happened?" Tony asked.

"I thought you were running interference for me."
Terry said.

"He must have snuck around me or something. Why didn't you hit that guy back? He's not much bigger than you."

"I don't know. His punch came out of nowhere and I kind of folded. Why does this crap have to happen to me all the time!" Terry nearly started sobbing, part due to the booze and part due to all the pain he felt. "What am I going to do about Sonya man? I think I love her." He whined.

"I wouldn't expect much from her now man. Women like guys who are manly. You dropped the ball."

"Just get me home Tony." Terry said. "Just get me home."

Terry went home that night and slept in late. When he got up his stomach muscles were painfully sore. He went downstairs and his parents had already gone out and so he got the phone directory and looked for gyms. He found one that claimed to be the best kickboxing gym in town, wrote down the address and phone number and drove down to check it out. The place was in kind of a rough part of town but the building was well kept up. When he got there, there was an older Chinese man sweeping the sidewalk and he asked him if the owner was in. He was surprised to learn the skinny old man was the owner and he was invited in.

"You want to join my gym? What do you want to learn?" Was the first thing the old man asked him.

"I want to learn to fight."

MUSTANG SUMMER LEIF GREGERSEN

"Fighting is easy. Anyone can teach you fighting, what you seem to want to learn is how to win fights."

"That's kind of the point isn't it?" Terry asked.

"I can only teach you how to train your body to find peace. Peace in motion, peace in your spirit. I will not take you on as a student."

"But why? I can pay you as much as it takes." Terry said.

"You are a young man at war. I can tell you drank last night, tell you got into a fight and lost, it is in your walk, your mannerisms." The old man spoke slowly, thoughtfully, as though he were weighing each word. "I see a lot of people like you, I can't train you, you are better off to train yourself. You can work out here, but without my help."

"Okay then, sell me a membership." Terry wanted to tell the old man about Brock, about Sonya. He wanted to tell him that he was a good guy deep down and wanted to do the right thing. But he held all his feelings inside. It was hard to tell if the lousy feeling he had in his stomach was from the punch he got or from how he felt about himself right at that moment.

Over the next weeks Terry went to the Shadow Warrior Gym as it was called, every day. He tried to go there early at first and then while he was using a weight bench for some barbell lifts another weightlifter came and started setting up some stuff right in his way without saying anything. If Terry had done his lifts properly this guy would have been hit in the head and would likely have ripped Terry into little pieces. So he started to come later in the day and there was a guy with long hair and a beard who would use the bench press set for an hour. Finally he settled into a routine, going there at lunch hour, when all there was for traffic was a few businesspeople on the treadmills and stationary bikes.

When Terry started coming at lunch he learned a new thing about the owner, who everyone called Si-Fu. He learned the gentle skinny old man was vicious. He ran a noon-time kickboxing class and while Terry was riding the exercise bike, running on the treadmill, skipping rope and lifting all the weights he could, there was constant screaming, shouting and thumps and bangs coming from the room where the classes were held. Sometimes when he had a break, he would look in and he noticed that the whole class would go through breathing and meditating before and after each session and that things got damned realistic at times. This was the kind of thing he wanted to try, this was what he felt would change him.

Terry really wanted to try and figure out Si-Fu, so he talked to a couple of people around the gym about him and found out he had been in a communist prison in China for a number of years and had either escaped or was let out and came to Canada to build a new life free of the constraints of his home country. He also learned he was a devout Buddhist and though he was wealthy, he had little care for money. It was rumored he also owned a high-rise apartment building downtown and had a maintenance man, an office worker and then did all the sweeping himself, just to keep himself focused.

Terry began to read up on Buddhism and tried to find out all he could about Chinese kickboxing and discovered that

Si-Fu taught a style all his own, there was no other dojo that used his methods in North America. Soon, Terry started meditating with the class outside the door of the teaching room and after a while he went inside and Si-Fu didn't object to him being there. After a while, Terry became engrossed in the feeling of completeness that meditating gave him and did it at home as well. As his learning and mindfulness progressed, Terry started casting off the things in his life he didn't need. He sold his car, he gave his stereo and TV to Tony. In a short while, all he would do was work out, go to work at the gas station and sleep. Still though, thoughts of Sonya crowded his head, while he was awake and while he was sleeping, in his dreams.

Finally, after he had completed his third month at Shadow Warrior, Si-Fu asked him to join him in his office. Si-Fu's office was filled with photos of military service, diplomas, awards, and even a couple of trophies from martial arts tournaments. He motioned for Terry to sit and then finally spoke:

"Terry, I have watched a change come over you these past months. You have been working very hard and you are progressing."

"Thank you." Terry said.

"I would like very much if you would join my class as a full member, but first I need to know your motivations for doing so."

"I just want to stop being a coward, stop feeling I can't stand up for myself or go out in public."

MUSTANG SUMMER   LEIF GREGERSEN

"Tell me Terry, do you still live with your mother and your father?"

"Yes. But I don't see why that matters..."

"Just tell me-is your father a strong and brave man, does he know how to fight?"

"No, not really. He's an engineer. He mostly works with plans and a computer."

"Those are your father's weapons. We live in a very safe society Terry. We don't all need to be warriors. There needs to be more kindness, more compassion or we will all eat ourselves apart from within. That is what meditation is about, this is what I teach. I do not teach violence and destruction. The people here are athletes, not warriors. Shadow Warrior means we fight by staying out of the light. We go around trouble, we don't look for it."

"All I know Si-Fu is that I will never have love, never have the girl I dream of, never be able to stand up to people unless I get stronger."

"You have a girl in mind?"

"In a way, yes."

"You are just a young man..."

"The problem is that I am not a man, I'm a cowardly boy. I want to be a man, I want to grow up finally and be able to protect those I love."

"I will let you join my class, but I think in the end you will find something you weren't looking for. Keep your eyes and your heart and mind open."

The next weeks went past and Terry went to the martial arts class each day, Si-Fu taught him more than he thought he could learn, about balance, strength, avoidance, disarming techniques. He grew stronger and stronger, then out of the blue leaving the gym one day he ran into Sonya.

"Hey Terry! Wow, you look great!" She said with a smile. He smiled back broadly, still wishing he hadn't left her at the dance with Brock last fall.

"Yeah, been working out, taking martial arts. You look pretty awesome yourself." He could hardly believe he let the words out like he did.

"What else have you been doing? I thought maybe you moved away, no one saw your car around, no one saw you in school."

"Oh, I've been working at the Turbo station in Inglewood. Also, I sold my car. Other than that, not much. How are you doing with Brock?"

"Can't seem to get rid of him no matter how hard I try." When she said this, Terry could see a deep sadness in her eyes, then they lit up again like it had never happened and she said, "Hey, I'll stop in for a coffee some time at your station. When do you usually work?" Terry nearly fell over himself, but somehow he rolled with it and said,

"Oh, Tuesdays and Thursdays after five for sure. Be nice to see you." Terry said confidently.

"Yeah, you too. Bye." Sonya waved and smiled and Terry melted inside.

That Tuesday Sonya came by and for the first time since they had met they actually talked. The station wasn't busy and so they went on about their favorite teachers, what they liked to read in their spare time and Terry impressed Sonya with his knowledge of Buddhism. She came again the next Tuesday and the next. Then Terry didn't see her for a week and wondered if anything had gone wrong. He called her up and she answered the phone and when she heard his voice she started crying.

"Hey, what's going on? Why are you so upset?"

"B... Brock found out about me coming to see you and he got really mad." She paused and Terry could hear more sobbing. "He said I can't see you anymore." Then before he could reply, she hung up the phone. Terry went out the front door and started running to her house, even though it was three miles away and mostly uphill. He got to Sonya's house within half an hour and her car was there and so he rang the doorbell. Her Dad answered.

"Hi Mister Tucker, I'm Terry, I'm a friend of Sonya's."

"Sonya is a little upset right now, I don't know if she wants to see anyone."

"Dad?" Sonya said from behind him. "Who's at the door?"

"Some boy named Terry. Do you want to see him?" She walked up to the door and Terry nearly went white. Sonya had a black eye.

"Sonya, what the hell is going on? Did Brock do this?"

"No, I got in a fight with a girl at school." From behind him, Sonya pointed at her Dad and put her finger to her lips, letting him understand she didn't want him to know who had really hit her.

"Terry, I think you had better go. You can call Sonya tomorrow when she's feeling better." Sonya's Dad closed the door and Terry felt a rage boiling up inside of him. He started walking towards Brock's neighborhood and it was like he had his own personal storm cloud walking with him. Just as he got near to Brock's house he saw Sonya's car pull up alongside him.

"Terry! Don't fight him, you can't win!" She said through the open car window. Terry didn't look at her or change his gait.

"I'm not going to fight him, I'm going to talk to him."

"He doesn't understand talking. He's taking these injections that make him crazy."

"Brock!" Terry yelled at the top of his voice as he neared his destination. "Come out now you useless son of a bitch!" Brock appeared at the front entrance to his house.

"What do you want goof boy?" Brock said.

MUSTANG SUMMER   LEIF GREGERSEN

"I want to lay down the law for you. I want you to come out here and have me go over what you are and are not allowed to do." Terry said.

"Nobody tells me what to do." Brock said and walked out to meet Terry. As soon as he got in close he yelled, "Punk ass bitch!" and gave Terry a shove. Terry stepped back with the assault, and in doing so maintained his balance.

"First off, you are going to turn yourself in for assaulting this young lady." Terry said, and Brock took a swing at his head which he dodged deftly.

"Second of all, you are going to leave Sonya be, you are no longer her boyfriend." Brock swung and missed again, this time nearly falling. "Anything you want to do or say to her you can do to me." Brock charged at Terry, catching him off guard and the two went tumbling onto the sidewalk. They grappled but Terry was the weaker of the two, though faster, but Brock got on top of him. He started punching Terry who dodged the odd blow, but took a couple to the face. Sonya began screaming for him to stop and started hitting his back. He turned to push her away and Terry flipped him and put an arm lock on him from behind, pulling both arms straight out backwards and ground Brock's face into the pavement as he laid there helpless. Soon, the sound of sirens could be heard and Sonya ran to direct them to the pair of young men. She explained what had gone on and that Brock was on steroids and had hit her and picked a fight with Terry, who now had blood running down his face from his nose.

Terry and Sonya both pressed charges against Brock and he was put into a youth detention centre. Wounds healed and the two teenagers got to be good friends. As time passed Terry came to the realization that what he felt for Sonya was just a crush, not the true, deep real love that people usually don't experience until they are a little older. He had a long talk with Si-Fu about it and Si-Fu smiled at him and became the first adult he ever knew to go right out and say that he was proud of him. Soon, another year of school came and this time Terry was ready to move on. When he got his letter accepting him into University, he knew that life was going to work out for him that he had conquered all his demons.

THE END

Made in the USA
San Bernardino, CA
18 February 2020

64539450R00117